# Getting Started with the Internet of Things

**Cuno Pfister**

O'REILLY

BEIJING · CAMBRIDGE · FARNHAM · KÖLN · SEBASTOPOL · TAIPEI · TOKYO

# Getting Started with the Internet of Things
## by Cuno Pfister

Published by O'Reilly Media, Inc.
1005 Gravenstein Highway North, Sebastopol, CA 95472

O'Reilly books may be purchased for educational, business, or
sales promotional use. Online editions are also available for most
titles (*http://my.safaribooksonline.com*). For more information,
contact our corporate/institutional sales department:
800-998-9938 or *corporate@oreilly.com*.

**Print History:** May 2011: First Edition.

**Editor:** Brian Jepson
**Production Editor:**  Jasmine Perez
**Copyeditor:** Marlowe Shaeffer
**Proofreader:** Emily Quill
**Compositor:** Nancy Wolfe Kotary
**Indexer:** Angela Howard
**Illustrations:** Marc de Vinck
**Cover Designer:** Marc de Vinck

ISBN: 978-1-4493-9357-1

# Contents

# Preface

One of the most fascinating trends today is the emergence of low-cost *microcontrollers* that are sufficiently powerful to connect to the Internet. They are the key to the *Internet of Things*, where all kinds of devices become the Internet's interface to the physical world.

Traditionally, programming such tiny *embedded* devices required completely different platforms and tools than those most programmers were used to. Fortunately, some microcontrollers are now capable of supporting modern software platforms like .NET, or at least useful subsets of .NET. This allows you to use the same programming language (C#) and the same development environment (Visual Studio) when creating programs for small embedded devices, smartphones, PCs, enterprise servers, and even cloud services.

So what should you know in order to get started? This book gives one possible answer to this question. It is a *Getting Started* book, so it is neither an extensive collection of recipes (or design patterns for that matter), nor a reference manual, nor a textbook that compares different approaches, use cases, etc. Instead, its approach is "less is more," helping you to start writing Internet of Things applications with minimal hassle.

## The Platforms

The *.NET Micro Framework* (NETMF) provides Internet connectivity, is simple and open source (Apache license), has hardware available from several vendors, and benefits from the huge .NET ecosystem and available know-how. Also, you can choose between Visual Studio (including the free Express Edition) on Windows, and the open source Mono toolchain on Linux and Mac OS X.

There is an active community for NETMF at *http://www.netmf.com/ Home.aspx*. The project itself is hosted at *http://netmf.codeplex.com/*.

*Netduino Plus (http://www.netduino.com/netduinoplus)* is an inexpensive NETMF board from *Secret Labs (http://www.secretlabs.com)*. This board makes Ethernet networking available with a price tag of less than $60. It has the following characteristics:

» A 48 MHz Atmel SAM7 microcontroller with 128 KB RAM and 512 KB Flash memory

» USB, Ethernet, and 20 digital I/O pins (six of which can be configured optionally for analog input)

» Micro SD card support

» Onboard LED and pushbutton

» Form factor of the Arduino (*http://www.arduino.cc/*); many Arduino *shields* (add-on boards) can be used

» .NET Micro Framework preprogrammed into Flash memory

» All software and hardware is open source

There is an active community for the Netduino Plus (and NETMF) at *http://forums.netduino.com/.* All the examples in this book use the Netduino Plus.

# How This Book Is Organized

The book consists of three parts:

» Part I, Introduction

The first part tells you how to set up the development environment and write and run a "Hello World" program. It shows how to write to output ports (for triggering so-called *actuators* such as LED lights or motors) and how to read from input ports (for *sensors*). It then introduces the most essential concepts of the Internet of Things: HTTP and the division of labor between clients and servers. In the Internet of Things, devices are programmed as clients if you want them to push sensor data to some service; they are programmed as servers if you want to enable remote control of the device over the Web.

» Part II, Device as HTTP Client

The second part focuses on examples that send HTTP requests to some services—e.g., to push new sensor measurements to the Pachube service (*http://www.pachube.com*) for storage and presentation.

» Part III, Device as HTTP Server

The third part focuses on examples that handle incoming HTTP requests. Such a request may return a fresh measurement from a sensor, or may trigger an actuator. A suitable server-side library is provided in order to make it easier than ever to program a small device as a server.

» Appendix A, Test Server

This contains a simple test server that comes in handy for testing and debugging client programs.

» Appendix B, .NET Classes Used in the Examples

This shows the .NET classes that are needed to implement all examples, and the namespaces and assemblies that contain them.

» Appendix C, Gsiot.Server Library

This summarizes the interface of the helper library `Gsiot.Server` that we use in Part III.

# Who This Book Is For

This book is intended for anyone with at least basic programming skills in an object-oriented language, as well as an interest in sensors, micro-controllers, and web technologies. The book's target audience consists of the following groups:

» Artists and designers

You need a prototyping platform that supports Internet connectivity, either to create applications made up of multiple communicating devices, or to integrate the World Wide Web into a project in some way. You want to turn your ideas into reality quickly, and you value tools that help you get the job done. Perhaps you have experience with the popular 8-bit Arduino platform (*http://www.arduino.cc/*), and might even be able to reuse some of your add-on hardware (such as shields and *breakout boards*) originally designed for Arduino.

» Students and hobbyists

You want your programs to interact with the physical world, using mainstream tools. You are interested in development boards, such as the Netduino Plus, that do not cost an arm and a leg.

» Software developers or their managers

You need to integrate embedded devices with web services and want to learn the basics quickly. You want to build up an intuition that ranges from overall system architecture to real code. Depending on your prior platform investments, you may be able to use the examples in this book as a starting point for feasibility studies, prototyping, or product development. If you already know .NET, C#, and Visual Studio, you can use the same programming language and tools that you are already familiar with, including the Visual Studio debugger.

To remain flexible, you want to choose between different boards from different vendors, allowing you to move from inexpensive prototypes to final products without having to change the software platform. To further increase vendor independence, you probably want to use open source platforms, both for hardware and software. To minimize costs, you are interested in a platform that does not require the payment of target royalties, i.e., per-device license costs.

If your background is in the programming of PCs or even more powerful computers, a fair warning: embedded programming for low-cost devices means working with very limited resources. This is in shocking contrast with the World Wide Web, where technologies usually seem to be created with utmost inefficiency as a goal. Embedded programming requires more careful consideration of how resources are used than what is needed for PCs or servers. Embedded platforms only provide small sub-sets of the functionality of their larger cousins, which may require some inventiveness and work where a desired feature is not available directly. This can be painful if you feel at home with "the more, the better," but it will be fun and rewarding if you see the allure of "small is beautiful."

# What You Need to Get Started

This book focuses on the interaction between embedded devices and other computers on the Internet, using standard web protocols. Its examples mostly use basic sensors and actuators, so it is unnecessary to buy much additional hardware besides an inexpensive computer board. Here is a list of things you need to run all the examples in this book:

» A Netduino Plus board (*http://www.netduino.com/netduinoplus*)

» A micro USB cable (normal male USB-A plug on PC side, male micro USB-B plug on Netduino Plus side), to be used during development and for supplying power

» An Ethernet router with one Ethernet port available for your Netduino Plus

» An Internet connection to your Ethernet router

» An Ethernet cable for the communication between Netduino Plus and the Ethernet router

» A potentiometer with a resistance of about 100 kilohm and through-hole connectors

» A Windows XP/Vista/7 PC, 32 bit or 64 bit, for the free Visual Studio Express 2010 development environment (alternatively, you may use Windows in a virtual machine on Mac OS X or Linux, or you may use the Mono toolchain on Linux or Mac OS X)

------------------------------------------------------------------------

NOTE: There are several sources where you can buy the hardware components mentioned above, assuming you already have a router with an Internet connection:

» Maker SHED (*http://www.makershed.com/*)

   » Netduino Plus, part number MKND02
   » Potentiometer, part number JM2118791

» SparkFun (*http://www.sparkfun.com/*)

   » Netduino Plus, part number DEV-10186

- » Micro USB cable, part number CAB-10215 (included with Netduinos for a limited time)
- » Ethernet cable, part number CAB-08916
- » Potentiometer, part number COM-09806

For more sources in the U.S. and in other world regions, please see *http://www.netduino.com/buy/?pn=netduinoplus*.

---

It is also possible to add further sensors and actuators.

# Conventions Used in This Book

The following typographical conventions are used in this book:

» *Italic*

Indicates new terms, URLs, email addresses, filenames, and file extensions.

» `Constant width`

Used for program listings, as well as within paragraphs to refer to program elements such as variable or function names, data types, statements, and keywords.

» **`Constant width bold`**

Shows commands or other text that should be typed literally by the user.

» `Constant width italic`

Shows text that should be replaced with user-supplied values or by values determined by context.

---

NOTE: This style signifies a tip, suggestion, or general note.

---

# Using Code Examples

This book is here to help you get your job done. In general, you may use the code in this book in your programs and documentation. You do not need to contact us for permission unless you're reproducing a significant portion of the code. For example, writing a program that uses several chunks of code from this book does not require permission. Selling or distributing a CD-ROM of examples from O'Reilly books does require permission. Answering a question by citing this book and quoting example code does not require permission. Incorporating a significant amount of example code from this book into your product's documentation does require permission.

We appreciate, but do not require, attribution. An attribution usually includes the title, author, publisher, and ISBN. For example: *"Getting Started with the Internet of Things*, by Cuno Pfister. Copyright 2011 Cuno Pfister, 978-1-4493-9357-1."

If you feel your use of code examples falls outside fair use or the permission given here, feel free to contact us at *permissions@oreilly.com*.

# How to Contact Us

Please address comments and questions concerning this book to the publisher:

O'Reilly Media, Inc.
1005 Gravenstein Highway North
Sebastopol, CA 95472
800-998-9938 (in the United States or Canada)
707-829-0515 (international or local)
707-829-0104 (fax)

We have a web page for this book, where we list errata, examples, and any additional information. You can access this page at:

*http://oreilly.com/catalog/0636920013037*

To comment or ask technical questions about this book, send email to:

*bookquestions@oreilly.com*

For more information about our books, conferences, Resource Centers, and the O'Reilly Network, see our website at:

*http://oreilly.com*

# Safari® Books Online

 Safari Books Online is an on-demand digital library that lets you easily search over 7,500 technology and creative reference books and videos to find the answers you need quickly.

With a subscription, you can read any page and watch any video from our library online. Read books on your cell phone and mobile devices. Access new titles before they are available for print, and get exclusive access to manuscripts in development and post feedback for the authors. Copy and paste code samples, organize your favorites, download chapters, bookmark key sections, create notes, print out pages, and benefit from tons of other time-saving features.

O'Reilly Media has uploaded this book to the Safari Books Online service. To have full digital access to this book and others on similar topics from O'Reilly and other publishers, sign up for free at *http://my.safaribooksonline.com*.

# Acknowledgments

My thanks go to Brian Jepson, Mike Loukides, and Jon Udell, who made it possible to develop this mere idea into an O'Reilly book. It was courageous of them to take on a book that uses a little-known software platform, bets on a hardware platform not in existence at that time, and addresses a field that is only now emerging. Brian not only edited and contributed to the text, he also tried out all examples and worked hard on making it possible to use Mac OS X and Linux as development platforms.

I would like to thank my colleagues at Oberon microsystems for their support during the gestation of this book. Marc Frei and Thomas Amberg particularly deserve credit for helping me with many discussions, feedback, and useful code snippets. Their experience was invaluable, and I greatly enjoyed learning from them. Marc's deep understanding of REST architecture principles and its implementation for small devices was crucial to me, as was Thomas's insistence on "keeping it simple" and his enthusiasm for maker communities like those of Arduino and Netduino. Both showed amazing patience whenever I misused them as sounding boards and guinea pigs. I could always rely on Beat Heeb for hardware and firmware questions, thanks to his incredible engineering know-how, including his experience porting the .NET Micro Framework to several different processor architectures.

Corey Kosak's feedback made me change the book's structure massively when most of it was already out as a Rough Cut. This was painful, but the book's quality benefited greatly as a result.

I have profited from additional feedback by the following people: Chris Walker, Ben Pirt, Clemens Szyperski, Colin Miller, and Szymon Kobalczyk. I am profoundly grateful because their suggestions definitely improved the book.

The book wouldn't have been possible without the Netduino Plus, and Chris Walker's help in the early days when there were only a handful of prototype boards. Whenever I had a problem, he responded quickly, competently, and constructively. I have no idea when he finds time to sleep.

Last but not least, many thanks go to the team at Microsoft—in particular Lorenzo Tessiore and Colin Miller—for creating the .NET Micro Framework in the first place. Their sheer tenacity to carry on over the years is admirable, especially that they succeeded in turning the platform into a true open source product with no strings attached.

# I/Introduction

Thanks to the unrelenting progress of the semiconductor industry, all the digital parts of a computer can be put onto a single chip, called a *micro-controller*. A 32-bit microcontroller chip costing less than $10 may have more than twice as much memory as the original 8-bit Apple II computer with its 48 KB of RAM, and may run 100 times faster. A hobbyist board that incorporates such a chip, along with Ethernet and a Micro SD card slot, can be purchased for about $60.

Because of such inexpensive hardware and easy-to-use development platforms, it is now possible for hobbyists to create systems that interact with the physical world in every conceivable way. For example, a sensor can measure the humidity in a flowerpot, and a computer-controlled valve (actuator) lets water pass into the pot when the humidity drops too low.

Moreover, since the hardware allows the use of standard Internet protocols, monitoring and controlling can be done over the Internet. Various Internet services can be used for storing data, visualizing it, sharing it with other people, etc. For example, to learn about seasonal effects on humidity, you can store measurements of your flowerpot's humidity over the course of a year.

While these possibilities are fascinating and promising, there is also something creepy about the potential for devices to spy on our every move. This provides another reason why we should try to learn how such systems work. This understanding is, or at least ought to be, the basis for thinking about privacy policies that will become necessary sooner or later.

In Part I, I will show you how to set up the development environment so that you can start playing with simple sensors and actuators. Then I will lay the groundwork for Parts II and III, which show how you can program devices as clients that send requests to various services, or as servers that handle requests from clients, e.g., from web browsers.

# 1/Hello World

To familiarize you with the development environment, your first program should be a simple HelloWorld. Because the Netduino Plus board does not have a display, use the USB connection between board and development PC to write the string Hello World to the development environment's Output window running on the PC, as illustrated in Figure 1-1. The USB connection is used to deploy and debug your programs, and in the HelloWorld example, it allows you to send the Hello World string to your development PC.

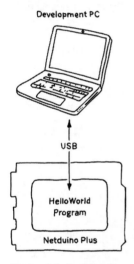

*Figure 1-1. Architecture of HelloWorld example*

## Setting Up the Development Environment

Before writing your first program for the .NET Micro Framework, you need to install a few tools and libraries, including:

» Microsoft Visual Studio 2010 or later. The free Visual Studio Express version is sufficient. Full commercial versions can also be used, of course. For my descriptions and screenshots, I will use Visual Studio Express. If you use Visual Studio Express, you must install the C# edition from *http://www.microsoft.com/express/Downloads*.

» Microsoft .NET Micro Framework 4.1 SDK or later, available at *http://www.netduino.com/downloads/MicroFrameworkSDK.msi*. (See *http://www.netduino.com/downloads/* for more information on compatible SDKs.)

» Your development board's SDK and drivers. The SDK and drivers for the Netduino Plus can be downloaded from *http://www.netduino.com/downloads/*.

» The client-side `Gsiot.PachubeClient` library and the server-side `Gsiot.Server` library, which are used in some of this book's examples. They can be downloaded from *http://www.gsiot.info/download/*.

All these software packages are free. The above tools require Windows XP, Vista, or Windows 7.

---------------------------------------------------------------------------

NOTE: Support for Mac and Linux should be available by the time this book is in print. For the latest updates, see *http://forums.netduino.com/*.

---------------------------------------------------------------------------


# HelloWorld

The `HelloWorld` program (Example 1-1) contains a class `HelloWorld` with a parameterless static method `Main`.

The keywords `public static void` specify the type of the method; in this case, it's `public` (is visible to other classes), `static` (doesn't need an instance of the `HelloWorld` class to execute the method), and `void` (doesn't return a value). Also, because the parentheses are empty, `Main()` doesn't expect you to pass it any arguments (objects or variables that would be referred to within the method).

In fact, you won't call `Main()` on your own; NETMF does it for you. When the Netduino Plus reboots or is powered on, it looks for the `Main()` method and runs it as the *entry point* of your program. This program writes the string `Hello World` to a debug console, e.g., the Output window of Visual Studio.

### Example 1-1. HelloWorld program

```
using Microsoft.SPOT;

public class HelloWorld
{
    public static void Main()
    {
        Debug.Print("Hello World");
    }
}
```

NETMF provides a `Debug` class in the `Microsoft.SPOT` namespace. `Debug`'s `Print` method writes text output directly to the development environment via the same *transport* (connection) used for deploying software to the device and for debugging. On the Netduino Plus board, it is a USB transport. Other development boards may use a serial transport (RS-232) or an Ethernet transport.

# Building the Program in Visual Studio

Assuming you have already installed the .NET Micro Framework SDK and the Netduino SDK, there are a few steps you must follow before you can type in the `HelloWorld` program:

1. Start Visual Studio.

2. Click on File→New Project....

3. Select Micro Framework in the Installed Templates pane, select Netduino Plus Application in the middle pane, and type HelloWorld in the Name field at the bottom (see Figure 1-2). Then click OK.

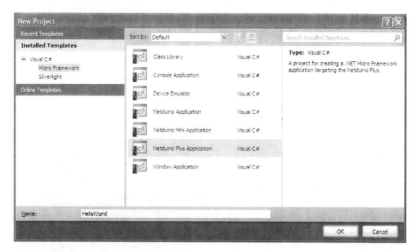

Figure 1-2. New Project dialog box

4.  In the Solution Explorer on the right side, double-click on *Program.cs*.
    A tab with the title Program.cs will open, containing some boilerplate
    program text.

5.  Replace the text with the HelloWorld program from Example 1-1.

6.  Select Debug→Build Solution to build the solution. At the bottom-left
    corner of Visual Studio, it should now say "Build succeeded".

# Deploying to the Device

Once you have built the example, you can deploy it to your hardware.
First, you need to make sure that the deployment properties are set as
shown in Figure 1-3. To do this, perform the following steps:

1.  In the Solution Explorer, right-click on the HelloWorld project (just below
    the text "Solution 'HelloWorld' (1 project)"), then select Properties in the
    menu. The tab shown in Figure 1-3 will open.

*Figure 1-3. Project properties*

2. On the left side, click on the .NET Micro Framework tab, which results in the dialog box shown in Figure 1-4. Make sure that the properties are set up as follows:

» Configuration: Active (Debug)

» Platform: Active (Any CPU)

» Transport: USB

» Device: select your Netduino from the drop-down list.

» Generate native stubs for internal methods: unchecked

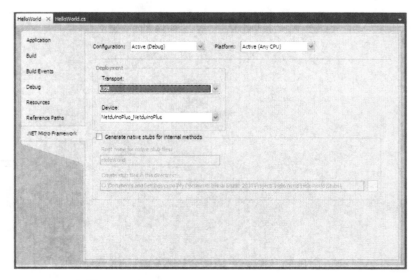

*Figure 1-4. .NET Micro Framework properties*

3. If the Device list box says <none>, you need to plug in your Netduino Plus.
   The first time you plug it in, the driver should be installed automatically.
   Its name should appear when you click on the Device list box.

4. To open the Output window, which will show debug output, use the key-
   board shortcut Ctrl-W, followed by O.

5. Next, select Debug→Start Debugging, and the `HelloWorld` program will
   be sent to your board, loaded by the .NET Micro Framework, after which
   the `Main` method is executed. The program then terminates immediately.

You can see the debug output in Visual Studio. The end of the output
should look something like this:

```
The thread '<No Name>' (0x2) has exited with code 0 (0x0).
Hello World
The thread '<No Name>' (0x1) has exited with code 0 (0x0).
The program '[1] Micro Framework application: Managed' has exited
    with code 0 (0x0).
```

Now you have successfully deployed your first program to a real device! It
is certainly not an Internet of Things application yet, as it does not involve
any communication over the Internet. Nor is it an embedded application,
as it doesn't use any of the typical embedded inputs or outputs (which we
will look at in the following chapters).

NOTE: If there is a problem during deployment, pull the USB cable out of your PC. If a dialog box with the text "There were deployment errors. Continue?" appears, click on the No button. Rebuild the program. Then plug in the USB cable again and immediately click Debug→Start Debugging. In some rare circumstances (usually involving complicated programs), the device seems to get really stuck, and a power cycle doesn't help. In those cases, it may help to erase your program from the Netduino Plus using the following steps:

1. Start up the MFDeploy tool (described in Chapter 6) and make sure USB is selected.

2. Unplug your Netduino Plus, then plug it back in while holding down the onboard button.

3. Release the button and then press the Erase button on the MFDeploy tool.

# 2/Writing to Actuators

You can now write your first truly embedded program. In a time-honored tradition, this program, `BlinkingLed`, which is the embedded equivalent of `HelloWorld`, makes an LED blink.

In Figure 2-1, the large box indicates a Netduino Plus, which has a blue LED—labeled LED on the board—that can be controlled from an application program. This LED is connected to a general-purpose input/output (GPIO) pin of the microcontroller. Most microcontrollers have a number of such GPIO pins, each of which can be configured as digital input or digital output. A digital output might be connected to an LED, as in our example; a digital input might be connected to a switch or button.

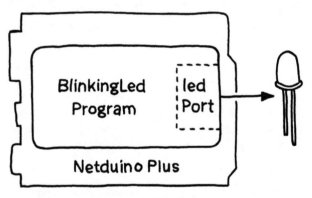

*Figure 2-1. Architecture of BlinkingLed*

## BlinkingLed

The `BlinkingLed` program, shown in Example 2-1, contains a simple endless loop that switches the LED on, waits for half a second, switches the LED off again, waits for another half a second, and then starts all over.

# Example 2-1. BlinkingLed

```
using System.Threading;
using Microsoft.SPOT.Hardware;
using SecretLabs.NETMF.Hardware.NetduinoPlus;

public class BlinkingLed
{
    public static void Main()
    {
        var ledPort = new OutputPort(Pins.ONBOARD_LED, false);

        while (true)
        {
            ledPort.Write(true);      // turn on LED
            Thread.Sleep(500);        // wait 500 ms

            ledPort.Write(false);     // turn off LED
            Thread.Sleep(500);        // wait 500 ms
        }
    }
}
```

The calls to the Sleep method in the Thread class make the program pause for (at least) a given number of milliseconds (a millisecond is 1/1000th of a second). In the .NET Micro Framework, using Thread.Sleep is the best practice for waiting, as it allows the hardware to go into a lower-power state to conserve energy.

---

NOTE: In many .NET programs, you'll see the developer specify a type name (such as OutputPort) for variable declarations. To simplify things, in this book I use the var keyword for all variable declarations where the type is obvious, such as:

» If the variable is initialized with a literal value (number, string).

» For an object created through its constructor (because you'll always see its class name on the right side of the expression, as is the case in this example).

» When a type cast is used (see the section "C#: Protecting You from Dangerous Conversions" in Chapter 12).

In all other cases, I use the type name to make the variable's type unambiguous and obvious—even if you read this book "on paper."

---

# C# Namespaces

In C#, related classes are bundled together into so-called *namespaces*. In the `BlinkingLed` program, the namespace `Microsoft.SPOT.Hardware` provides the class `OutputPort`. Its full name is `Microsoft.SPOT.Hardware.OutputPort`. Of course, you could spell out the full name of the class every time you use it, but for the sake of readability and convenience, it is often preferable to use a *using directive*. If you specify the directive `using Microsoft.SPOT.Hardware;` (as I did in `BlinkingLed`) at the beginning of your program, you can use the short name `OutputPort`, rather than the full name. I will use short names in this book; please see the tables in Appendix B to find the appropriate namespace for each class used in these examples.

---

NOTE: The "SPOT" in several NETMF namespaces stands for *Smart Personal Object Technology*, originally developed for programmable personal devices such as watches. The .NET Micro Framework grew out of these activities.

---

## Running the Program

To run the program, create a new Netduino Plus Application project in Visual Studio, and replace the contents of *Program.cs* with the code given in Example 2-1. Next, build it and deploy it to your Netduino Plus, as described in the section "Deploying to the Device" in Chapter 1.

## Digital Outputs

In the .NET Micro Framework, using a physical pin as output is represented by an *output port* object, which is an instance of the class `OutputPort`.

An output port provides the method `Write` that takes the target state of the output pin as a Boolean (`true` or `false`) parameter. Using such an output port, called `ledPort` in Example 2-1, the LED can be switched on by writing the value `true`, and switched off by writing the value `false`.

When I defined the output port `ledPort`, I specified the microcontroller pin that is connected to the LED. In this case, I want to use the built-in (onboard) LED.

Pins are represented by the type `Cpu.Pin`, but you don't specify the number of the pin you want to use. Instead, manufacturers provide constants for the pins on their boards. On a Netduino Plus, you must specify `Pins.ONBOARD_LED` for the onboard LED's pin. In this book, we are mainly interested in the constants shown in Table 2-1, where I also include some *input ports* to be used in later chapters. These pins are defined in the namespace `SecretLabs.NETMF.Hardware.NetduinoPlus`, which is provided as part of the Netduino SDK. When you type in `Pins.`, Visual Studio conveniently pulls up a list of all the available pins on a Netduino Plus.

**Table 2-1. Pin assignment of Netduino board (excerpt)**

| Connected hardware | Pin usage | Constant |
|---|---|---|
| Onboard LED (blue) | Digital output | Pins.ONBOARD_LED |
| Onboard switch | Digital input | Pins.ONBOARD_SW1 |
| Pins D0 through D13 | Digital input or digital output | Pins.GPIO_PIN_D0 to Pins.GPIO_PIN_D13 |
| Pins A0 through A5 | Analog input[1] | Pins.GPIO_PIN_A0 to Pins.GPIO_PIN_A5 |

[1] Alternatively, these pins can be configured as digital inputs or as digital outputs.

------------------------------------------------------------------------

NOTE: Many super bright blue and white LEDs can tolerate the 3.3V GPIOs that the Netduino Plus uses. You can connect such an LED to any of the GPIO pins: the long lead (positive) goes to the GPIO pin, and the short lead (negative) goes to the board's ground pin. However, if you are using an LED of another color, note that it prefers a lower voltage; therefore, you should put a 220 ohm resistor between one of the LED's leads (either one is OK) and your board.

------------------------------------------------------------------------

The second parameter of the `OutputPort` constructor shown in Example 2-1 indicates whether the LED should initially be switched on or off. In our case, `false` indicates that it should be off at the beginning.

A pin may be used with at most one output (or input) port at the same time—i.e., creating a port object reserves this pin. Attempts at reserving a pin multiple times will lead to an *exception*, which is a software event that is triggered by an error condition. Unless you create handlers that catch and resolve exceptions, they will typically cause your Netduino Plus program to halt.

# 3/Reading from Sensors

The first example in this chapter, `LightSwitch`, not only writes to output ports, it also reads from input ports. The switch input is used to control the LED output, as shown in Figure 3-1. While the switch (actually a push button on the Netduino Plus board) is closed, the LED stays lit; otherwise, it is dark.

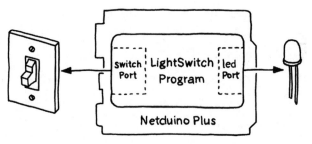

*Figure 3-1. Architecture of LightSwitch*

## LightSwitch

The program `LightSwitch` (Example 3-1) reads the current switch state periodically and copies it to the LED. This is done frequently enough that a user does not detect a delay when she opens or closes the switch. Delays of 1/10th of a second or less are undetectable by humans; therefore, the loop is executed every 100 milliseconds.

------------------------------------------------------------------------

NOTE: A value read from a sensor—in this case, the switch or button—is called a *measurement* or *sample*. The time span between two subsequent measurements is called the *sampling period*.

------------------------------------------------------------------------

## Example 3-1. LightSwitch

```csharp
using System.Threading;
using Microsoft.SPOT.Hardware;
using SecretLabs.NETMF.Hardware.NetduinoPlus;

public class LightSwitch
{
    public static void Main()
    {
        var switchPort = new InputPort(Pins.ONBOARD_SW1, false,
            Port.ResistorMode.Disabled);
        var ledPort = new OutputPort(Pins.ONBOARD_LED, false);

        while (true)
        {
            bool isClosed = switchPort.Read();
            if (isClosed)
            {
                ledPort.Write(true);
            }
            else
            {
                ledPort.Write(false);
            }
            Thread.Sleep(100);                  // 100 milliseconds
        }
    }
}
```

------------------------------------------------------------------------

NOTE: Since the first branch of the `if (isClosed)` statement is executed if
`isClosed` is `true`, and the other branch is executed if `isClosed` is `false`, the
entire if statement can be completely replaced by the following statement:

```csharp
ledPort.Write(isClosed);
```
------------------------------------------------------------------------

To build the program, create a new Netduino Plus project, name it
LightSwitch, and replace the contents of *Program.cs* with the code in
Example 3-1. Next, build the project and deploy it to your Netduino Plus,
as described in the section "Deploying to the Device" in Chapter 1.

## Digital Inputs

For reading the switch state, create object `switchPort` of type `InputPort` for the pin to which your board's switch is connected (in this case, I use the `ONBOARD_SW1` constant to refer to the pin that's wired to the Netduino's built-in switch). When an input port is created, you have to pass two parameters in addition to the pin number: `bool glitchFilter` and `Port. ResistorMode resistor`.

Parameter `glitchFilter` determines whether button presses are debounced—i.e., whether intermittent mechanical contacts are suppressed. In `LightSwitch`, it doesn't really matter whether a value is read that is "wrong" temporarily; therefore, I pass `false`. This would be different if the application did something critical whenever the button was pressed, like launching rockets. In such a situation, you wouldn't want one keypress to launch an entire salvo of rockets, simply because the button jumps up and down a bit before it settles down.

To understand the `resistor` parameter, we need to look at the hardware of the board. The microcontroller's input pin `ONBOARD_SW1` is connected to *power* (PWR)—i.e., to the supply voltage on the one hand—and via switch SW1 to *ground* (GND), or to zero voltage. Without resistance between power and ground, it would be unclear what the input pin would see when the switch is closed (Figure 3-2). Power? Ground? Something in between?

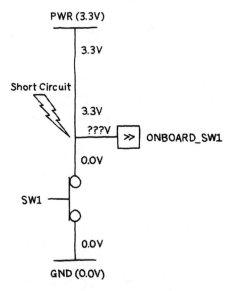

*Figure 3-2. Why a resistor is needed*

Moreover, the current would become infinite when the switch is closed—in other words, you would get a short circuit that might destroy the board. These are the reasons why a resistor R must be supplied. It limits the current, prevents a short circuit, and defines whether ONBOARD_SW1 detects a high or a low voltage. On the Netduino Plus board, this *pull-up resistor* is placed between ONBOARD_SW1 and power. Figure 3-3 shows an excerpt of *board schematics* that illustrates the situations with switch SW1 open (left) and closed (right).

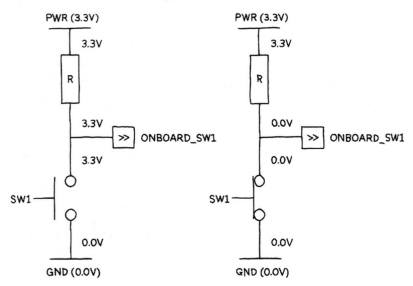

Figure 3-3. Switch open (left) and switch closed (right)

------------------------------------------------------------

NOTE: The simple rectangular shape of a resistor, as shown in Figure 3-3, is used in many countries. In the U.S., it is more common to use the following symbol:

------------------------------------------------------------

Because the Netduino Plus board already provides a pull-up resistor for `ONBOARD_SW1`, the microcontroller pin doesn't need to provide additional resistance of its own. Therefore, the value `Port.ResistorMode.Disabled` is passed as a parameter to the input port constructor.

---

NOTE: If there were no external pull-up resistor on the board, you would have to pass `Port.ResistorMode.PullUp` to enable the microcontroller's internal pull-up resistor. This is relevant if you use one of the digital inputs on the Netduino Plus connectors to connect an external switch.

---

If the switch is open—i.e., the button is released—the supply voltage causes the pin to "see" a high voltage (Figure 3-3, left). If the switch is closed—i.e., the button is pressed—the voltage below the resistor is sucked down to ground, causing the pin to "see" a zero voltage (Figure 3-3, right).

## Positive and Negative Logic

It would be nonintuitive if an input port with switch semantics returned `true` for an *open* switch, so the Netduino GPIO driver makes sure that `switchPort.Read` returns `false` for an open switch (high voltage), and `true` for a closed switch (low voltage). However, be aware that if you use other GPIO ports with switches and pull-up resistors attached, they will return `true` for open switches. This is because the framework cannot know the desired semantics in advance, and therefore it cannot adjust other ports than `ONBOARD_SW1` for this *negative logic*!

The board schematics in Figure 3-3 are simplified because on the Netduino, the same switch is used as a reset button if it's not used as a GPIO port, which requires additional logic not shown here. Without this logic, `SW1` and `R` could have been swapped, turning `R` into a *pull-down resistor*. This would have avoided the use of negative logic.

The reason why hardware is often designed with pull-up resistors instead of pull-down resistors is historical: earlier circuit technologies had built-in pull-up resistors. With today's CMOS circuits, there is no technical reason anymore, but the tradition of using a mix of positive and negative logic unfortunately remains.

# VoltageReader

Reading digital inputs for buttons, switches, and the like is fine, but sometimes you may want to read *analog* inputs as well. The `VoltageReader` in Figure 3-4 shows how this can be done.

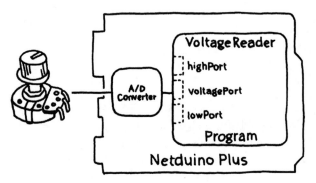

*Figure 3-4. Architecture of VoltageReader*

The complete code is given in Example 3-2. It polls a *potentiometer* every three seconds and prints the raw value and the corresponding voltage value to the debug output.

-----------------------------------------------------------------------

NOTE: If you develop on Mac OS X or Linux, the debug output can be sent over a serial line instead of USB. For more information, please see the Mono forum at http://forums.netduino.com/.

-----------------------------------------------------------------------

## Example 3-2. VoltageReader

```
using System.Threading;
using Microsoft.SPOT;
using Microsoft.SPOT.Hardware;
using SecretLabs.NETMF.Hardware;
using SecretLabs.NETMF.Hardware.NetduinoPlus;

public class VoltageReader
{
    public static void Main()
    {
```

```csharp
const double maxVoltage = 3.3;
const int maxAdcValue = 1023;

var voltagePort = new AnalogInput(Pins.GPIO_PIN_A1);
var lowPort = new OutputPort(Pins.GPIO_PIN_A0, false);
var highPort = new OutputPort(Pins.GPIO_PIN_A2, true);

while (true)
{
    int rawValue = voltagePort.Read();
    double value = (rawValue * maxVoltage) / maxAdcValue;
    Debug.Print(rawValue + "   " + value.ToString("f"));
    Thread.Sleep(3000);                 // 3 seconds
}
    }
}
```

---

NOTE: Note the string conversion `value.ToString("f")`. The optional format string parameter `"f"` indicates a fixed-point number representation with two digits after the decimal point.

---

To run the program, first connect a potentiometer to your Netduino Plus, as shown in Figure 3-5.

---

NOTE: Revision A boards require that you first connect **Aref** and **3V3** before you can use analog inputs. On Revision B boards or later, this is no longer necessary (but is allowed).

The potentiometer should have a resistance of about 100 kilohm, and it should have through-hole connectors arranged in a row so that it can be stuck directly into the Netduino Plus connector.

---

Next, create a new Netduino Plus project, name it VoltageReader, and replace the contents of *Program.cs* with the code in Example 3-2. Then, build the project and deploy it to your Netduino Plus, as described in the section "Deploying to the Device" in Chapter 1.

To view the output, choose Debug→Windows→Output. Every three seconds you'll see a new value displayed in the window.

## Analog Inputs

A typical analog sensor translates some physical phenomenon, such as temperature, into a voltage level. The *analog/digital converter* (ADC) built into the microcontroller of the Netduino Plus can measure this voltage and turn it into an integer number. For an ADC with 10-bit *resolution*, like the one in the Netduino Plus, the numbers range from 0 (for 0.0 Volt) to 1023 (for 3.3 Volt). These are the 1,024 values that can be represented with 10 bits ($2^{10}$ values). An ADC supporting only 8 bits would yield the 256 numbers between 0 and 255 ($2^8$ values); an ADC supporting 12 bits would yield the 4,096 numbers between 0 and 4095 ($2^{12}$ values).

A Netduino Plus provides six analog inputs on one of the blue connectors. They are labeled `Analog In, 0` to 5. If you have a suitable potentiometer, you can stick it into the Netduino Plus connector such that one of the outermost leads (no matter which one) connects to `A0`, the other outermost lead connects to `A2`, and the middle lead connects to `A1`. See Figure 3-5 for an image of this scenario.

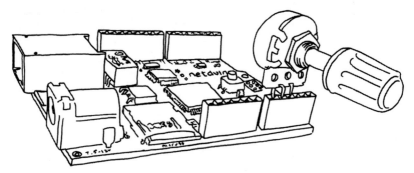

*Figure 3-5. Netduino Plus with potentiometer*

Because the pins on our potentiometer lie so closely together, it is convenient to plug them directly into the row of analog pins on the Netduino. However, we will not be configuring all the connected pins to be analog inputs. Recall that the analog pins on the Netduino can be used either for general-purpose digital I/O or for analog input. In our case, we will configure the pins at the two ends (A0 and A2) to be digital outputs supplying 3.3V on one pin and 0.0V on the other. Only the middle pin (A1) will be configured to be an analog input.

Figure 3-6 shows a schematic diagram for this arrangement of components.

GPIO_PIN_A2 (3.3V)

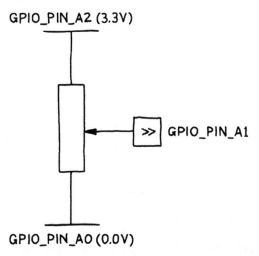

GPIO_PIN_A0 (0.0V)

*Figure 3-6. Potentiometer connected to three microcontroller pins*

The symbol for a potentiometer looks similar to a resistor because it is indeed a kind of variable resistor. Depending on how you turn the potentiometer's knob, the resistances between pins A0 and A1 on the one hand, and between pins A1 and A2 on the other hand, will change. As a result, the voltage seen by A1 will change, all the way from 0.0 Volt to 3.3 Volt. A potentiometer can therefore be regarded as a variable *voltage divider*, as shown in Figure 3-7.

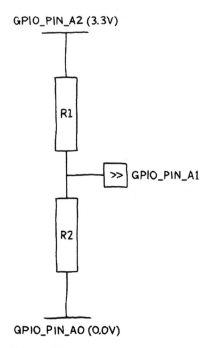

GPIO_PIN_A2 (3.3V)

R1

>> GPIO_PIN_A1

R2

GPIO_PIN_A0 (0.0V)

*Figure 3-7. Potentiometer as a variable voltage divider*

With your potentiometer attached to the Netduino Plus, you have hands-on experience with an analog sensor. This is a good basis for learning about more advanced sensors later on. After all, most analog sensors produce varying voltages that the Netduino measures at one of the analog inputs, representing them as an unsigned integer value.

Let's take another look at part of Example 3-2:

```
const double maxVoltage = 3.3;
const int maxAdcValue = 1023;

var voltagePort = new AnalogInput(Pins.GPIO_PIN_A1);
var lowPort = new OutputPort(Pins.GPIO_PIN_A0, false);
var highPort = new OutputPort(Pins.GPIO_PIN_A2, true);
```

From the microcontroller's ADC resolution (adcResolution), which is 10 bit, the maximum value of the input port is 1023. The analog input port for pin A1 is an instance of class AnalogInput.

Pins **A0** and **A2** are used as digital outputs here, forcing one of them to low (**false**) and the other to high (**true**). The Netduino Plus allows the use of pins **A0** to **A5** as either analog inputs, or as digital inputs *or* outputs (i.e., as GPIOs). This trick lets you use one pin as voltage (high corresponds to 3.3 Volt) and one as ground (0.0 Volt).

Reading an analog input port is accomplished with this line:

```
int rawValue = voltagePort.Read();
```

This yields a value between 0 and 1023. Scaling it to between 0.0 and 3.3 Volt is done in the following way:

```
double value = (rawValue * maxVoltage) / maxAdcValue;
```

We multiply the value we read (**rawValue**) by the maximum voltage (3.3) and divide it by the maximum value possible (1023).

---

## Voltage Divider

A voltage divider produces an output voltage that is a fraction of its input voltage. In Figure 3-7, the output voltage seen at **GPIO_PIN_A1** is 3.3V * (R2 / (R1 + R2)). A potentiometer allows you to change R2 by turning its knob.

Other sensors have their resistances changed through other physical effects. For example, brightness affects the resistance of a photo resistor.

---

# II/Device as HTTP Client

In this part, we will see how devices can be programmed as HTTP clients, accessing services on the Internet. The main focus will be on Pachube, a service created specifically for Internet of Things applications. Your device(s) can send measurements to Pachube for storage and for later access via web browsers or other programs.

The .NET Micro Framework provides mainly two application programming interfaces (APIs) for implementing HTTP clients: the high-level `HttpWebRequest` API (in namespace `System.Net`) and the low-level `Socket` API (in namespace `System`). You will learn how to work with either one, depending on your application needs and available hardware resources.

# 4/The Internet of Things

Now that you have seen how to work with simple sensors and actuators, it is time to take the next step toward an Internet of Things application. In this chapter, I will briefly introduce the Internet of Things, and the related *Web of Things*.

The Internet of Things is a global network of computers, sensors, and actuators connected through Internet protocols.

A most basic example is a PC that communicates over the Internet with a small device, where the device has a sensor attached (e.g., a temperature sensor), as shown in Figure 4-1.

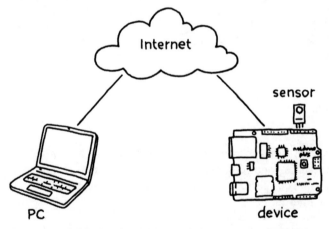

*Figure 4-1. A PC and a device connected through the Internet*

The *TCP/IP* protocol is the key Internet protocol for such communication scenarios. It enables the transfer of byte streams between two computers in either direction. For example, using the TCP/IP protocol, the device in Figure 4-1 may periodically deliver temperature measurements to a program running on the PC.

# HTTP

While it is possible to run any kind of proprietary protocol on top of TCP/IP, there are a few popular and widely supported standard protocols. If you use a standard protocol to deliver your sensor data, you'll be able to work with many more devices and applications than if you developed your own proprietary protocol.

The most important standard protocol by far is the *Hypertext Transfer Protocol* (HTTP), the protocol of the World Wide Web. HTTP describes how a client interacts with a server, by sending *request messages* and receiving *response messages* over TCP/IP, as diagrammed in Figure 4-2.

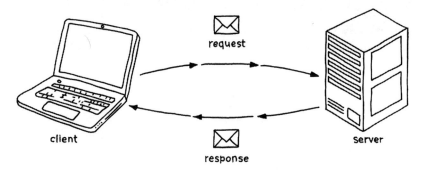

*Figure 4-2. Client sends request message, server answers with response message*

Web browsers are the most popular HTTP clients, but you can easily write your own clients—and your own servers. If you use a web browser to access a device, the device has the role of a web server, providing a *web service* over the Internet.

A server contains *resources*, which can be anything of interest, e.g., a document (typically an HTML web page), the most current measurement of a sensor, or the configuration of a device. When you design a web service, you need to decide which resources it should expose to the world.

HTTP uses *Uniform Resource Identifiers* (URIs) to tell the server which resource the client wants to read, write, create, or delete. You know URIs from web browsing; they look something like these:[1]

```
http://www.example.com/index.html
http://www.example.com/temperatures
http://www.example.com/temperatures/actual
http://www.example.com:50000/temperatures/actual
http://www.example.com/temperatures?alarm=none
http://www.example.com/temperatures?alarm=high
http://www.example.com/temperatures?alarm=low
http://www.example.com/valve/target
```

A URI indicates the *scheme* (e.g., http), the *host* (e.g., www.example.com), optionally the *port* (e.g., 50000), and the *path* (e.g., /temperatures/actual) to the resource owned and managed by this host, as shown in Figure 4-3. Optionally, a URI may also contain a *query* (e.g., alarm=high) after a ? character that follows the path.

For the HTTP protocol, port 80 is used by default unless another port is chosen explicitly, perhaps for testing purposes. The path is called *request URI* in HTTP; it denotes the target resource of an HTTP request.

---

NOTE: URIs that start with a scheme are *absolute URIs*. URIs without a scheme are *relative URIs*. A request URI is a relative URI that starts with /. Sometimes you will have to work with absolute URIs and other times with relative URIs, as you will see in the examples.

---

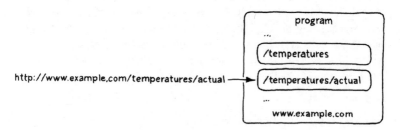

*Figure 4-3. URI that addresses a resource managed by a host*

---

[1] These URIs are URLs (*Uniform Resource Locators*) as well. A URL is a URI that also indicates a specific location of a resource, in addition to its identity. I will use the more general term URI throughout this book.

There are several kinds of HTTP requests that a client can send, but the most popular are *GET* for reading a resource, *PUT* for writing to a resource, *POST* for creating a resource, and *DELETE* for deleting a resource. Web browsers mostly issue GET requests, which make up the vast majority of HTTP requests. In a Web of Things application, a GET request to a URI, such as:

```
http://www.example.com/temperatures/actual
```

may return the most recent measurement of a temperature sensor, while a PUT to a URI, such as:

```
http://www.example.com/valve/target
```

may change the setting of an actuator—in this case, a valve. POST requests add sub-resources to a resource, which is similar to putting a file into a directory. For example, a POST of a measurement to the following resource:

```
http://www.example.com/temperatures
```

may create a new resource:

```
http://www.example.com/temperatures(42135)
```

A DELETE request removes a resource—e.g., it may remove the /temperatures resource:

```
http://www.example.com/temperatures
```

from the server. (Of course, this would not physically remove the temperature sensor from the hardware.)

PUT requests, POST requests, and GET responses carry *representations* of the addressed resource. The best-known representation is the *Hypertext Markup Language*, better known as HTML. A web browser is an HTTP client that knows how to render HTML pages on the screen. There are other popular representations: PDF, JPEG, XML-based data formats, etc. A web service may support *one or several representations* for a single resource. For example, a temperature measurement may be represented in a plain-text representation, like this:

```
23.5 deg
```

or in an XML representation, like this:

```
<sample>
    <value>23.5</value>
    <unit>deg</unit>
</sample>
```

Some representations are standardized, like HTML, but you may also define your own representations, like those above. Some representations are self-contained documents; others support *links* to other resources. You know the hypertext links from HTML, which use URIs to address other resources. By clicking on a link, you cause the browser to send a GET request to obtain a representation of that resource. This request is sent to the host contained in the link's URI.

Let's look at a complete example of an HTTP request/response interaction (Figure 4-4):

1.  This diagram shows a GET request, as it may be sent by a web browser or your own client program. The client requests a representation of the resource's "actual temperature as measured by the temperature sensor," whose URI consists of the host `www.example.com` and the request URI `/temperatures/actual`.

2.  The service at host `www.example.com` receives the request, measures the temperature, and returns a response message. In this example, the response indicates success (`200 OK`) and a plain-text representation that is 8 bytes long. The representation is `23.5 deg`.

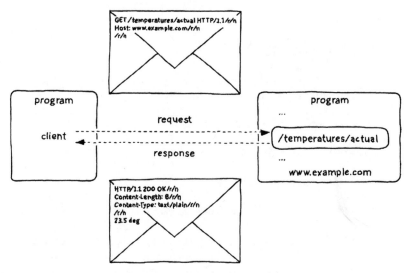

*Figure 4-4. HTTP request and response*

Even the most complex web interactions consist of such message exchanges. The Web includes several hundred million clients and several hundred thousand servers with their resources, and it produces a torrent of messages that carry resource representations. The technical term for this architecture is *representational state transfer*, or *REST*. For more information on REST, see *RESTful Web Services* by Leonard Richardson and Sam Ruby (O'Reilly).

The focus of *Getting Started with the Internet of Things* is to show how REST and common web standards can be used as the preferred way of creating Internet of Things applications. Such applications are sometimes called Web of Things applications, to emphasize the use of web standards on top of the basic Internet protocols.

The Web of Things consists of RESTful web services that measure or manipulate physical properties.

Thus, the term Web of Things focuses on the application layer and the real-world "things" that are measured or manipulated. The term Internet of Things focuses on the underlying network layers and the technical means for measuring and manipulating the physical environment—i.e., sensors and actuators.

# Push Versus Pull

There are four basic ways in which your device may communicate with another computer on the Web:

1. Device is the *client*, pushing data *to* a server

2. Device is the *client*, pulling data *from* a server

3. Device is the *server*, providing data *to* clients

4. Device is the *server*, accepting data *from* clients

These patterns can be visualized as shown in Figure 4-5. A black arrow indicates the direction of a request message and a dotted arrow indicates the direction in which data flows, i.e., in which direction a resource representation is sent.

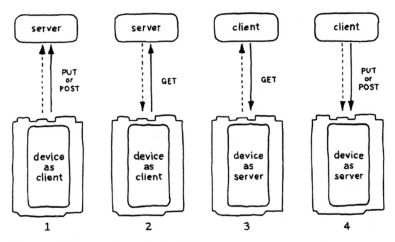

*Figure 4-5. Four basic web interaction patterns*

In monitoring applications, a device *produces* data, i.e., measurements from its attached sensors. For such applications, the interaction patterns 1 and 3 are suitable: data flows from the device *to* another computer; the device is either client (1) or server (3).

In control applications, a device *consumes* data, i.e., commands from a web browser or other client. For such applications, the interaction patterns 2 and 4 are suitable: data flows to the device *from* another computer; the device is either client (2) or server (4).

---

NOTE: A web browser is a client that mainly pulls data from web servers by sending GET requests to them. So you are probably most familiar with interaction pattern 2 because this is the way web browsers work.

---

In Part II, I will focus on the device as client (i.e., on scenarios 1 and 2). Since in general, a device cannot know in advance when you want to send it a command (e.g., to set up an actuator or to reconfigure a sensor), it makes sense to support devices as servers as well. Therefore, I will discuss scenarios 3 and 4 in Part III. I believe that the potential of the Internet of Things will only be realized if devices can become clients, servers, or both.

# 5/Pachube

Imagine that your Netduino Plus uses a sensor to take measurements periodically. After each measurement, the Netduino Plus immediately sends the sample to a server for storage and later retrieval. This server effectively provides a *feed* resource to which you publish your data samples. You may already know the concept of feeds from RSS feed readers. A feed entry can be anything of interest, from political news to blog entries to measurements, as in the case of your Netduino Plus. In a way, a feed that contains measurements can be thought of as a news source about the physical world.

For such an example, you need a suitable web service to which your device can send its measurements. Conveniently, there's a free service, Pachube, which does exactly this. It provides web-based interfaces for storing and for accessing feeds, as shown in Figure 5-1.

*Figure 5-1. Example of a Pachube feed*

NOTE: The example in Figure 5-1 is a NASA feed. It is atypical insofar as the source of its data is a multimillion dollar space probe—not exactly a low-cost device. Nevertheless, you can use Pachube just as well with your $60 Netduino Plus.

To use Pachube, you need a free account and a feed to which you can send your own data. Follow these steps to create both the account and a first feed:

1. Sign up for a free account at *http://www.pachube.com/signup*.

2. On the "my settings" page (*http://www.pachube.com/users/ <your account name>/settings*), you will find the private master API key that you will need later on in your Pachube client programs.

NOTE: Your Netduino Plus programs will send the API key along with every HTTP request to Pachube. The API key tells Pachube that your client program is authorized to add new measurements to your feeds. You'll see how to use this in Chapter 6.

Pachube also supports more advanced *secure sharing keys* as a more secure and fine-grained mechanism where you can, for example, use keys specifically for particular applications, limit the actions possible with these keys, control how long they remain valid, etc.

3. Set up your first feed at *http://www.pachube.com/feeds/new*.

4. For the Feed type, click on "manual".

5. For the Feed title, type in a suitable name, such as "My first feed".

6. For the Feed tags, you could type in "gsiot" so that other readers of this book can find it.

7. For the Exposure, click on "indoor".

8. For the Disposition, click on "fixed".

9. For the Domain, click on "physical".

10. You may enter other information if you want, such as a location name and the location itself (click on the Google map to define the location). If you choose to provide a location, I suggest you pick a well-known public point of interest near you rather than your actual home address.

11. Note the ID of this feed. It is part of the web page URI (circled in Figure 5-2).

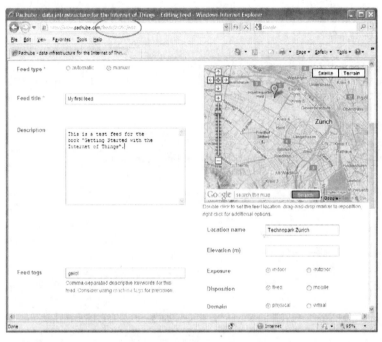

*Figure 5-2. Editing the properties of a Pachube feed*

------------------------------------------------------------------------

NOTE: A Pachube feed contains one or several *data streams*; for example, a feed may contain one data stream for every sensor in a building. In the simplest case, a feed has only one data stream—for the measurements of one sensor. In our examples, we will use two data streams: one for voltage values, the other for simple integer numbers.

------------------------------------------------------------------------

12. Click on "+ Add a new datastream". Enter "voltage" as the ID, enter "Volt" in the Units field, and enter V in the Symbol field. In Type, select "derived SI", which means that this is a unit derived from some other physical units that are considered more basic.

13. Click on "+ Add a new datastream" again. Enter "number" as the ID and leave all other properties as they are.

14. Click on Save Feed.

15. Given your Pachube feed ID, look at the feed's home page by typing in its URI. For example, for the feed **256**, use the URI `http://www.pachube.com/feeds/256`.

Pachube supports a number of URIs for accessing a given feed or data stream. Table 5-1 shows the most important URIs, using the feed ID **256** and the data stream ID **0** as examples.

Table 5-1. Most important URIs for accessing Pachube feeds

| Pachube URI | Description |
| --- | --- |
| *http://www.pachube.com/feeds/256* | HTML home page of feed **256**. |
| *http://api.pachube.com/v2/feeds/256. json* | JSON (*http://www.json.org*) representation of feed **256**, providing maximum, minimum, and current measurement values, plus some metadata that describes the feed.<br><br>It is also possible to request the data in XML or CSV formats by using the `.xml` or `.csv` suffixes respectively, instead of `.json`. |
| *http://api.pachube.com/v2/feeds/256/ datastreams/0.csv?duration=24hours& interval=900* | History of measurements in data stream **0** of feed **256**, represented as comma-separated values. Can be imported directly into a spreadsheet. All measurements of the last 24 hours are given, in 15-minute intervals. You can vary the arguments to adjust the time period and the minimum interval between the points. |
| *http://api.pachube.com/v2/feeds/256/ datastreams/0.png?duration=24hours& interval=900* | Same data as in the above example, but represented as a diagram. |

In Chapter 6, you will learn how to send data to your Pachube feed from a program that runs on your Netduino Plus.

---

# JSON

*JSON*, which stands for *JavaScript Object Notation*, is a textual format for representing arbitrary data. In this respect, it is similar to the often-used XML representation. JSON is popular for web applications since its text is simpler and usually less verbose than equivalent XML text. While JSON is part of the JavaScript language, it is supported by libraries for practically all programming languages today, and has thereby gained "a life of its own." Here is an example of JSON text:

```
{
    "recorded_at" : "2011-03-23T13:29:37Z",
    "max_value" : 25.5,
    "min_value" : 0.0,
    "value" : 1.6
}
```

---

# 6/Hello Pachube

In this chapter, I will show a basic HTTP client, HelloPachube, that pushes samples to Pachube, as shown in Figure 6-1.

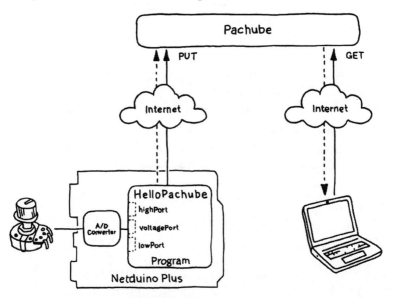

*Figure 6-1. Architecture of HelloPachube*

HelloPachube runs on the Netduino Plus and sends measurements to the Pachube web service by issuing HTTP PUT requests. The user, through his web browser, sends HTTP GET requests to Pachube to retrieve feed entries. The data flow originates in the device, goes up to Pachube, and continues from there to the user.

## Setting Up the Network Configuration

Before you can run such a client, you need to make sure that your Netduino Plus board has access to the Internet—i.e., it can send request messages to any server visible on the Internet. I assume that your

Netduino Plus is connected to the Internet via a router and a cable or DSL modem (Figure 6-2).[1] This means that you have a local area network to which both the board and your development PC are connected. During development and debugging, the PC and Netduino Plus are directly connected via a USB cable as well.

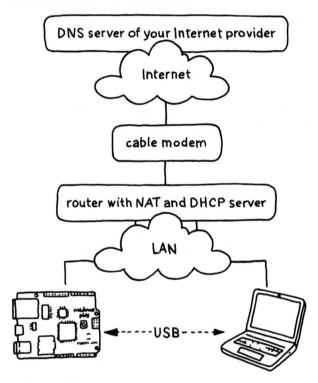

Figure 6-2. Connection of board to the Internet

## Internet Addresses

A router typically implements the *Dynamic Host Configuration Protocol* (DHCP). This protocol allows your development PC, your Netduino Plus, and other devices to automatically obtain *Internet addresses* (e.g., 192.168.0.3 for the PC, and 192.168.0.4 for the

---

[1] Sometimes a cable modem already includes a router in the same box.

Netduino Plus). The Internet protocols rely on Internet addresses for routing messages between clients and servers.

If your Netduino Plus obtains its Internet address automatically via DHCP, it typically gets an Internet address in one of these reserved address ranges:

    192.168.*xxx*.*xxx*
    172.16.*xxx*.*xxx*
    10.*xxx*.*xxx*.*xxx*

where *xxx* lies between 0 and 255. Public Internet servers never use these reserved addresses. They are unique only within a given local area network, not worldwide like other Internet addresses. For example, there are thousands of computers with the *private address* 192.168.1.100. This is not a problem as long as your device is only a client, but it can be a problem for devices used as servers, as we will see in Part III.

To implement such a multiplexing of Internet addresses, a router has to perform *network address translation* (NAT). This hides the private Internet addresses from the Internet by making it appear as though all Internet traffic from the board or from the development PC originated from the router. This provides a certain degree of security because a program on the Internet cannot directly address—and therefore try to connect to—a device hidden behind the router. In addition, it reduces the number of Internet addresses that must be visible globally, which is important because the common four-byte IPv4 Internet addresses will basically be used up by the time this book comes out.

A client program can directly use an Internet address to connect to a server on the Internet—e.g., the address 173.203.98.29 to connect to a Pachube server. Since such Internet addresses are not very convenient, you can alternatively use a *domain name* for addressing a host. In the above example, the domain name is pachube.com. Domain names are registered with the Internet's *domain name system* (DNS). The domain name system allows for looking up domain names, much in the same way as a phone book is used for looking up names (except instead of finding phone numbers, the domain name system returns Internet addresses). A domain name lookup is simply another request over the Internet, e.g., to a DNS server of your Internet service provider.

# The MFDeploy Tool

Before you can use your Netduino Plus on the network, you need to check its network settings and configure it if necessary. In particular, you should make sure that DHCP is switched on and that the correct *MAC address* of the board is set. The MAC address is a unique six-byte identifier, typically written like this:[2]

```
3c-8a-4a-00-00-07
```

To check or modify the network configuration, use the tool MFDeploy, which is provided as part of the Microsoft .NET Micro Framework SDK. To find it, click Start→All Programs→Microsoft .Net Micro Framework 4.1→Tools and run MFDeploy.exe. Another way to find it is to look in the directory:

```
C:\Program Files\Microsoft .NET Micro Framework\v4.1\Tools\
MFDeploy.exe
```

(On a 64-bit operating system, the first folder will be *Program Files (x86)*.)

Now, perform the following steps:

1. Start *MFDeploy.exe*. The dialog box .NET Micro Framework Deployment Tool opens.

2. In the leftmost Device list box, change the selection from Serial to USB.

3. Plug your Netduino Plus USB cable into your development PC. In the rightmost Device list box, the name NetduinoPlus_NetduinoPlus should appear.

4. Click on the Ping button to make sure the device responds. As result, the large text box should now show "Pinging... TinyCLR".

5. In the Target menu, select Configuration→Network. The Network Configuration dialog box opens.

6. If it isn't checked already, click on the DHCP checkbox to enable automatic configuration of most network parameters.

---

[2] You will find the MAC address of your Netduino Plus on the sticker at the bottom of the board.

7. If it isn't configured yet, enter your board's MAC address. This is the only parameter you need to provide. You can leave the DNS Primary Address and the DNS Secondary Address at 0.0.0.0, as shown in Figure 6-3.

8. Click the Update button.

9. Reboot your Netduino Plus. It should now automatically obtain the missing network parameters from your router. To make sure that the Netduino Plus reboots, I usually perform a complete power-off/power-on cycle by briefly unplugging and reinserting the USB cable from the PC. After such a power cycle, you have five seconds to deploy a new program; otherwise, the most recently deployed program is restarted automatically.

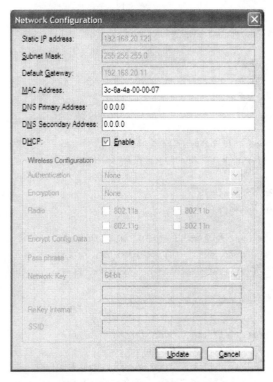

*Figure 6-3. Network Configuration in MFDeploy*

To check whether the configuration works correctly, run the `HelloPachube` client program described next.

# HelloPachube

Now that your Netduino Plus is ready to access the Internet, we can look at a first version of a Pachube client. Its source code is given in Example 6-1.

## Example 6-1. HelloPachube

```
using System;
using System.Threading;
using Gsiot.PachubeClient;
using Microsoft.SPOT;
using Microsoft.SPOT.Hardware;
using SecretLabs.NETMF.Hardware;
using SecretLabs.NETMF.Hardware.NetduinoPlus;

public class HelloPachube
{
    public static void Main()
    {
        const string apiKey = "your Pachube API key";
        const string feedId = "your Pachube feed id";
        const int samplingPeriod = 20000;    // 20 seconds

        const double maxVoltage = 3.3;
        const int maxAdcValue = 1023;

        var voltagePort = new AnalogInput(Pins.GPIO_PIN_A1);
        var lowPort = new OutputPort(Pins.GPIO_PIN_A0, false);
        var highPort = new OutputPort(Pins.GPIO_PIN_A2, true);

        while (true)
        {
            WaitUntilNextPeriod(samplingPeriod);
            int rawValue = voltagePort.Read();
            double value = (rawValue * maxVoltage) / maxAdcValue;
            string sample = "voltage," + value.ToString("f");
            Debug.Print("new message: " + sample);
            PachubeClient.Send(apiKey, feedId, sample);
        }
    }
}
```

```
static void WaitUntilNextPeriod(int period)
{
        long now = DateTime.Now.Ticks / TimeSpan.TicksPerMillisecond;
        var offset = (int)(now % period);
        int delay = period - offset;
        Debug.Print("sleep for " + delay + " ms\r\n");
        Thread.Sleep(delay);
    }
}
```

To run the program, follow these steps:

1. Make sure that your Netduino Plus is connected to your Ethernet router and that it is correctly configured for network access (see the previous section).

2. If you haven't done so already, download the Visual Studio project Gsiot. PachubeClient from *http://www.gsiot.info/download/*, unzip it, and put it into the *Visual Studio 2010\Projects\* directory.

3. Create a new Visual Studio project (using the Netduino Plus template) and name it HelloPachube. Replace the contents of *Program.cs* with the code from Example 6-1.

4. You must replace the strings for apiKey and feedId so they match your Pachube API key and feed ID.

5. Right-click on References in the Solution Explorer. Select Add→ New Reference. In the Add Reference dialog box, click on the Browse tab. In the directory hierarchy, go up two steps to directory *Project*. In the directory *Gsiot.PachubeClient*, open the subdirectory *Gsiot.Pachube-Client* (yes, the same name again). In this directory, open the *bin* subdirectory. From there, open the *Release* subdirectory. In this subdirectory, select the *Gsiot.PachubeClient.dll* file. Click the OK button. You have now added the assembly *Projects\Gsiot.PachubeClient\Gsiot.PachubeClient\ bin\Release\Gsiot.PachubeClient.dll*.

Now you're ready to test it: build the project and deploy it to your Netduino Plus, as described in the section "Deploying to the Device" in Chapter 1.

NOTE: In the simplest case, one C# namespace is translated into exactly one .NET assembly (stored in a DLL), which is the binary form of .NET code. For the .NET Micro Framework, a built-in postprocessor tool translates .dll assembly files into .pe files, which are a more compact representation of the same code. These are the files that get deployed to the Netduino Plus.

## Viewing the Results

After `HelloPachube` has started, you'll see something like the following in Visual Studio's Output window:

```
sleep for 19069 ms

The thread '<No Name>' (0x3) has exited with code 0 (0x0).
new message: voltage,0.06
time: 01/01/2009 02:16:40
memory available: 20136
Status code: 200
sleep for 19371 ms

The thread '<No Name>' (0x4) has exited with code 0 (0x0).
new message: voltage,0.06
time: 01/01/2009 02:17:00
memory available: 20136
Status code: 200
sleep for 19210 ms

The thread '<No Name>' (0x5) has exited with code 0 (0x0).
new message: voltage,1.52
time: 01/01/2009 02:17:20
memory available: 20136
Status code: 200
sleep for 19369 ms

The thread '<No Name>' (0x6) has exited with code 0 (0x0)....
```

Because a Netduino Plus has no battery-backed real-time clock, its clock is started anew whenever you reboot the device. Upon rebooting, the initial time is the start of January 1, 2009.

Twenty seconds pass between two consecutive samples; roughly 19 of them are spent sleeping. You can see that the samples were successfully sent to Pachube because the returned status code is 200, which is the OK status code of HTTP.

To verify that the samples have indeed arrived at Pachube, type the following URI into your web browser, replacing *your Pachube feed id* with your feed ID:

`http://www.pachube.com/feeds/your Pachube feed id`

You should now see that the status of your feed is marked as `currently: live`. This means that the most recent sample is not older than 15 minutes; otherwise, the status `currently: frozen` would be shown.

-------------------------------------------------------------------------------

NOTE: If you don't see this output, make sure that the Netduino Plus is connected via Ethernet cable to a router, and via USB cable to your development PC. Use MFDeploy to check whether DHCP is enabled and the MAC address is set. Check whether the example correctly builds and whether its properties are set up to deploy to the device via USB.

-------------------------------------------------------------------------------

To see a graphical representation of the most recent samples, view the feed's web page, look at the graph there, and click the label "last hour".

## How It Works

The initialization of the HelloPachube `Main` method starts with two Pachube-related constants: your Pachube API key (`apiKey`) and the ID of the feed to which you want to publish your samples (`feedId`). After that, there are a few other constants and variables that are set:

» Specifying how often to send updates

First comes the timing-related constant `samplingPeriod`. The goal for the example is to sample and publish a new observation at regular intervals, namely once every `samplingPeriod`, which is given in milliseconds (20,000 milliseconds is 20 seconds).

To publish a sample, send a web request and wait for its response. The time for such a complete *round-trip* consists of the time it takes for the request to travel to the server, for the server to create a response, and for the response to travel back to the client.

NOTE: The speed of the round-trip depends mainly on five factors: the distance between client and server, the current traffic on the Internet, the performance of the server, the current load of the server, and the amount of data transferred. Typical numbers range from about 50 milliseconds for round-trips to servers close to the client, to well over 1,000 milliseconds for round-trips across continents or to overtaxed servers (even for short messages). Since they depend on the Internet's current traffic, the times for subsequent round-trips from the same client to the same server can vary.

If you use a slower connection than Ethernet, this can also affect round-trip times. For example, if you dropped a Netduino out in the woods with a cheap 2G GSM module, it would probably spend most of the 20 seconds doing the round-trip.

» Setting up the voltage reader

The `voltagePort` object and related variables and constants are set up, as you saw in Chapter 3. They are used for reading voltage values from an attached potentiometer.

After the variables and constants are initialized, a `while` loop controls what happens from then on. This *main loop* will run until you turn off the Netduino Plus.

The main loop does basically three things:

» Sleeps until the next sample is due, using the helper method `WaitUntil-NextPeriod`, which I will discuss in the next section.

» Creates the sample by reading the voltage port.

» Sends the value to Pachube using `PachubeClient.Send`. This method takes the Pachube API key, your feed ID, plus the sample data, and sends them to Pachube in a suitable PUT request message. It then receives the response message and prints the response's status code to the debug console.

To use the `Gsiot.PachubeClient` for sending requests to Pachube in a "fire and forget" manner, you don't need to know more than this. However, if you want to know how the library actually works, how you could modify it, or how you could create a similar library, you need to understand more about how to send HTTP request messages and receive HTTP response messages. This is the topic of Chapter 7.

## The WaitUntilNextPeriod Method

In this example, samples should be taken at highly regular intervals. To do this, you can use the `WaitUntilNextPeriod` helper method, which you can reuse in similar programs later on. The following text explains the method in some detail. You can skip the explanation if you just want to go ahead and use the method.

After each sample is sent, the program needs to sleep until the next period starts. How can this delay be calculated with precision when we don't know in advance exactly how long it will take to send a request and receive its response?

This example starts a new period every 20 seconds. (Free Pachube accounts don't allow updates more often than every 12 seconds.) Assume the following:

» You last took a reading at 09:32:40.

» After the time it took you to send a message and receive the response, it is now 09:32:46.

» You want to send the next message (and start a new period) at 09:33:00.

The delay then can be calculated as the difference between the length of the period (20 seconds) and the offset, where the offset indicates how far you are into the current period. The offset is calculated as the current time (i.e., now) modulo the period. In the example shown in Figure 6-4, the offset is six seconds; therefore, the delay is 14 seconds.

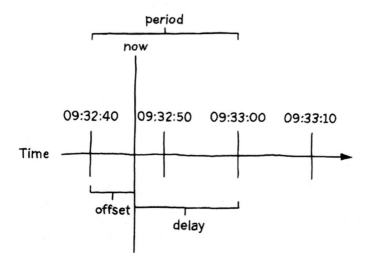

Figure 6-4. Calculating the delay until the start of the next period

The property DateTime.Now.Ticks gives the current time[3] in *ticks*, which in .NET is a time at a resolution of 100 nanoseconds. Dividing ticks by 10,000 (TimeSpan.TicksPerMillisecond) yields the same time in milliseconds, albeit less precisely. This requires a 64-bit long integer type. To calculate the modulus, use the % operator of C#. Because the result of a modulus operation is always smaller than the operand, in this case period, it can be safely cast to a 32-bit integer using the (int) cast.

------------------------------------------------------------------

NOTE: The modulo operator, %, computes the remainder of a division. For example, the division of 7 by 2 yields 3. Computing "backwards" by multiplying the result 3 by the divisor 2, we get 6. The difference between 6 and the dividend (7) is the remainder—in this case, 1.

------------------------------------------------------------------

WaitUntilNextPeriod ensures that sampling starts at highly regular intervals. It is robust even in cases where an iteration takes longer than its period allows for. This might occur if something unexpected happens, such as an exception that takes an inordinately long time to be sent to the debugger. This may result in one or several periods being skipped—but the next one starts at a correct period boundary anyway.

---

[3] On a Netduino, this is the time since the device has booted. It has no battery-backed real-time clock that keeps track of time when it isn't powered.

# What Netduino Said to Pachube

To see that there is no magic involved in HTTP requests, let's look at the data actually transferred to the Pachube server during a request:

```
PUT /v2/feeds/fid.csv HTTP/1.1\r\n
Host: api.pachube.com\r\n
X-PachubeApiKey: your Pachube API key is here\r\n
Content-Type: text/csv\r\n
Content-Length: 12\r\n
\r\n
voltage,1.52
```

This is the text sent over the Internet to Pachube! At least that's what is sent if the measured voltage is 1.52.

An HTTP request consists of one *request line*, followed by a number of *header lines*, followed by an empty line, and optionally followed by a *message body* (i.e., the message's *content*).

The request line starts with the HTTP method: PUT, GET, etc. After a blank, the request URI indicates the resource to be accessed. After another blank, the HTTP version is given, which is usually version 1.1 these days. The request line is terminated by a carriage-return byte followed by a newline byte.

NOTE: \r\n stands for the two bytes CR and LF (carriage return and line feed, respectively). If you were to look at the actual text of the request, they would not be visible.

HTTP defines a number of headers, both for requests and responses. For requests, the Host header is particularly important because it defines to which computer the request is sent—in this case, to api.pachube.com. If you take this host and the request URI in the request line (here, it's /v2/feeds/ fid.csv), you can construct the absolute URI of the resource accessed by this PUT request:

```
http://api.pachube.com/v2/feeds/fid.csv
```

Unlike the URIs that we have seen in Chapter 5, which have been URIs for consumers of Pachube feeds, this is a URI for producers that send measurements to Pachube.

Different applications may use very different sets of headers. For our purposes, the most important headers are Host (for requests only) and Content-Length and Content-Type (for both requests and responses). Applications may define their own headers, like the X-PachubeApiKey above. The order of HTTP headers is not significant, as every possible ordering is correct.

The message body consists of exactly the 12 bytes voltage,1.52 here, has no terminating characters, and is separated from the last header by an empty line.

------------------------------------------------------------------------

NOTE: To find out what exactly your client is sending, you may use a simple test server (such a server is given in Appendix A). To make Hello-Pachube send its requests to a test server running on your PC, change the constant baseUri in Gsiot.PachubeClient so that it points to your server.

------------------------------------------------------------------------

# What Pachube Said to Netduino

An HTTP response from Pachube may look like this:

```
HTTP/1.1 200 OK\r\n
Server: nginx/0.7.65\r\n
Date: Mon, 07 Feb 2011 13:36:55 GMT\r\n
Content-Type: text/plain; charset=utf-8\r\n
Connection: keep-alive\r\n
Set-Cookie: _pachube_app_session=BAh7BjoPc2Vzc2lvbl9...;\r\n
Cache-Control: max-age=0\r\n
Content-Length: 1\r\n
Age: 0\r\n
Vary: Accept-Encoding\r\n
```

In this response, the first line, known as the *status line*, is the most important. HTTP defines a number of status codes; status code 200 means that the request was handled successfully. (The most important status codes are given in Chapter 10.) The status code is located between the HTTP version and a plain-text version of the status code. The text version of the status code is optional—you neither need to generate nor interpret it. It is merely a convenience for human readers of HTTP interactions.

Responses may contain many headers, as you can see from this example. Fortunately, you can usually ignore almost all of them. Nevertheless, let's take a look at the headers in the response:

» `Server`

Indicates the web server software that Pachube uses.

» `Date`

Indicates the time when Pachube has sent the response.

» `Content-Type: text/plain; charset=utf-8`

Indicates the format of the Pachube response. In this case, it is plain text encoded in UTF8 (the most common encoding of Unicode characters).

» `Connection: keep-alive`

Is a relic from HTTP 1.0 (an early version of the HTTP specification). Originally, a new TCP/IP connection was opened for every request and then closed after the request. Because opening a connection incurs a considerable overhead, it is better to keep a connection open if requests are sent to the same server every couple of seconds. The `keep-alive` value was added to indicate this desire. It is not relevant anymore because most servers and clients today support HTTP 1.1, where connections are kept alive by default. However, if for any reason a client or a server wants to close a connection after a message exchange, it can signal this to the other party by including the `Connection: close` header.

» `Set-Cookie`

Indicates a cookie (some text that the server sends a client to store, and which the client will send to the server in future requests) with a session identifier. You can ignore cookies because they are not needed for our examples.

» `Cache-Control: max-age=0`

Is intended for managing caches between client and server. It indicates that this response must not be cached.

» `Content-Length: 1`

Indicates that the response message body consists of one byte.

» `Age: 0`

Is an estimate (in seconds) of the time it has taken to produce and transmit the response. It is a header produced by some intermediary cache between server and client. You can ignore it.

» `Vary: Accept-Encoding`

Tells the client that it may send an `Accept-Encoding` header along with GET requests, in order to ask for different representations of the resource. As we have seen in Chapter 5, Pachube supports several formats for samples: `csv`, `json`, png, etc. However, you won't need the `Accept-Encoding` header in the examples of this book. Instead, you can pass the desired format as part of the URI, e.g., `http://api.pachube.com/v2/feeds/256.csv`.

The message body, after the last `CR LF` (empty line), consists of exactly one blank character. It seems a bit strange that it is not completely empty in the case of Pachube, but you can usually ignore the message body of a PUT response anyway.

HTTP requests and responses are not complicated. Any device capable of supporting TCP/IP is able to send data to Pachube or to similar services.

# 7/Sending HTTP Requests—The Simple Way

HelloPachube in Chapter 6 is so simple because the `Gsiot.PachubeClient` library is built for the single purpose of pushing samples to Pachube. It completely hides the .NET classes needed to implement an HTTP client. If you want to use Pachube in a different way, or if you want to write clients for other services, you can use the more general `HttpWebRequest` and `HttpWebResponse` classes, which are located in the `System.Net` namespace.

## SimplePutRequest

Example 7-1 shows how these classes can be used to send a single sample to Pachube.

### Example 7-1. SimplePutRequest

```
using System.IO;
using System.Net;
using System.Text;
using Microsoft.SPOT;

public class SimplePutRequest
{
    public static void Main()
    {
        const string apiKey = "your Pachube API key";
        const string feedId = "your Pachube feed id";

        // this is the "sample" we want to send to Pachube
        var sample = "number,42";
        // convert sample to byte array
```

```
byte[] buffer = Encoding.UTF8.GetBytes(sample);

// produce request
var requestUri =
    "http://api.pachube.com/v2/feeds/" + feedId + ".csv";
using (var request = (HttpWebRequest)WebRequest.
    Create(requestUri))
{
    request.Method = "PUT";

    // headers
    request.ContentType = "text/csv";
    request.ContentLength = buffer.Length;
    request.Headers.Add("X-PachubeApiKey", apiKey);

    // content
    Stream s = request.GetRequestStream();
    s.Write(buffer, 0, buffer.Length);

    // send request and receive response
    using (var response = (HttpWebResponse)request.
        GetResponse())
    {
        // consume response
        Debug.Print("Status code: " + response.StatusCode);
    }
}
```

To run this example:

1.  Make sure your Netduino Plus is connected to your Ethernet router, and
    that it is correctly configured for network access (see Chapter 6).

2.  Create a new Visual Studio project (using the Netduino Plus template)
    and name it SimplePutRequest. Replace the contents of *Program.cs* with
    the code from Example 7-1.

3. You must replace the strings for *apiKey* and *feedId* so that they match your Pachube API key and feed ID.

4. Right-click on References in the Solution Explorer. Select Add→New Reference. In the Add Reference dialog box, click on the .NET tab (if it is not already selected). Locate System.Http in the list and click OK to add this assembly to your project.

---

### C# "using" Statements

Both `HttpWebRequest` and `HttpWebResponse` implement the `IDisposable` interface, which means that they provide `Dispose` methods. Instances of such types should be disposed after they have been created and used by calling their `Dispose` methods. (If you fail to create the object for some reason, `Dispose` cannot and need not be called.)

To prevent you from having to deal with this on your own, C# provides the `using` statement, which automatically calls `Dispose` at the end of the code block, even if an exception occurred:

```
using (var request = (HttpWebRequest)WebRequest.
    Create(requestUri))
{
    // set up request line parameters, headers, and content
    using (var response =
        (HttpWebResponse)request.GetResponse())
    {
        // consume response
    }
}
```

---

Now, you're ready to test it: build the project and deploy it to your Netduino Plus, as described in the section "Deploying to the Device" in Chapter 1.

A dummy "sample" is then defined and converted from a string to a byte array with a call to `Encoding.UTF8.GetBytes`. (When you need to convert in the other direction, use `Encoding.UTF8.GetChars` to obtain a character array, and then call `new string(charArray)`.)

When you look at your Pachube feed web page, you will notice that at the bottom of the page, data stream `number` has now appeared below data stream `voltage`.

# Making Web Requests

SimplePutRequest uses three classes from Microsoft's System.Net namespace: WebRequest, HttpWebRequest, and HttpWebResponse:

» **WebRequest**

A factory class (a class that generates other classes) whose method WebRequest.Create(requestUriString) creates an object that represents a request for the protocol indicated by the argument requestUriString. It issues a DNS lookup to find out the Internet address of the domain name given in the requestUriString. Alternatively, it accepts URIs that directly contain Internet addresses instead of domain names.

» **HttpWebRequest**

A complete HTTP request with its headers and body.

» **HttpWebResponse**

A complete HTTP response with its headers and body.

These classes are implemented in the System.Http assembly, providing support for clients of web services. When used, you need to reference them in your Visual Studio project.

---

NOTE: System.Http is a large assembly, taking up about two-thirds of the Flash memory available for your application code (on a Netduino Plus with the standard firmware), or roughly 46 KB.

---

## The HttpWebRequest Class

The method WebRequest.Create takes a URI string as an argument and creates a new object of type WebRequest. If the URI starts with http, the object it returns is a subclass of WebRequest, namely an HttpWebRequest. This means that a type cast can be used:

```
var request = (HttpWebRequest)WebRequest.Create(requestUri);
```

An `HttpWebRequest` object has several properties that correspond to elements of an HTTP request line or to some important HTTP headers. You need to set the following ones before you make the request:

» The `Method` property (in the example above, `request.Method`) represents the HTTP method; typically, this is `GET`, `PUT` (as in Example 7-1), `POST`, or `DELETE`. This value will be sent as part of the HTTP request line, which is the first line of an HTTP request.

» You must initialize the `ContentLength` property with the length of the request message body in bytes (not counting the request line and the request headers). This value will be sent as the `Content-Length` header of the request message.

» You must initialize the `ContentType` property with a string indicating the type of content you'll be sending. In Example 7-1, this was `text/csv`, which indicates you'll be sending comma-separated values. This value will be sent as the `Content-Type` header of the request message.

» Pachube requires that you authorize new samples by providing the `X-PachubeApiKey` header with your API key. Without a valid API key, Pachube does not accept new samples from a client. Because this is a nonstandard HTTP header, the method `Headers.Add` is used for adding it to the `request` object.

You also need to write the HTTP body to a byte stream, which has been created along with the `request` object. You'll obtain it by calling the request's `GetRequestStream` method. After writing the entire contents of the byte buffer that contains your sample into this stream, you need to close the stream. Fortunately, the `using` statement does this automatically.

----------------------------------------------------------------

NOTE: As for the connection management, it happens behind the scenes—i.e., `HttpWebRequest.GetResponse` automatically reuses an open connection to the host if one is available; otherwise, it creates a new connection. It keeps this connection open unless you have set `request.KeepAlive` to `false`, which sets the `Connection` header to `close` instead of the (redundant) `keep-alive`. If the *response* message contains a `Connection: close` header, the connection is closed as well.

----------------------------------------------------------------

Sending a request and receiving its response is combined in the request's GetResponse method:

```
var response = (HttpWebResponse)request.GetResponse();
```

## The HttpWebResponse Class

An object of type **HttpWebResponse** has several properties that correspond to elements of an HTTP status line or to some important HTTP headers, which are represented as properties of the object:

» StatusCode

   A numerical representation of the result.

» StatusDescription

   A textual representation of the result. It can be ignored; programs should rely on the StatusCode.

» ContentLength

   The length of the response message body in bytes.

» ContentType

   The type of the response message body.

» Headers

   A collection with the response headers.

To get access to the response message body itself, you must call the method GetResponseStream, which returns a stream object that is used to read the contents of the response message body.

One Read operation on the byte stream may or may not yield all of the HTTP content, depending on how the network protocol stack is implemented, as well as the timing of data packets on the Internet. To make sure the complete body is received, Read must be called in a loop as often as necessary until there is nothing left to read (see Example 7-2).

## Example 7-2. Reading from a stream

```
var buffer = new byte[response.ContentLength];
Stream stream = response.GetResponseStream();
int toRead = buffer.Length;
while (toRead > 0)
{
    // already read: buffer.Length - toRead
    int read = stream.Read(buffer, buffer.Length - toRead, toRead);
    toRead = toRead - read;
}
```

Before the loop, create a byte buffer with the exact length of the message body. So when the loop is entered, the entire buffer length still remains to be read (**toRead**). In every iteration of the loop, one or more bytes are read (**read**), and therefore the number of bytes left to read is reduced accordingly, until it reaches zero.

To demonstrate how more information from a response object could be accessed, Example 7-3 shows how to reconstruct the HTTP message and print it out to the debug console.

## Example 7-3. SimpleGetRequest

```
using System.IO;
using System.Net;
using System.Text;
using Microsoft.SPOT;

public class SimpleGetRequest
{
    public static void Main()
    {
        const string apiKey = "your Pachube API key";
        const string feedId = "your Pachube feed id";

        // produce request
        var requestUri =
            "http://api.pachube.com/v2/feeds/" + feedId + ".csv";
        using (var request = (HttpWebRequest)WebRequest.
            Create(requestUri))
        {
            request.Method = "GET";
```

```csharp
        // headers
        request.Headers.Add("X-PachubeApiKey", apiKey);

        // send request and receive response
        using (var response = (HttpWebResponse)request.
            GetResponse())
        {
            // consume response
            HandleResponse(response);
        }
    }
}

public static void HandleResponse(HttpWebResponse response)
{
    // response status line
    Debug.Print("HTTP/" + response.ProtocolVersion + " " +
                response.StatusCode + " " +
                response.StatusDescription);

    // response headers
    string[] headers = response.Headers.AllKeys;
    foreach (string name in headers)
    {
        Debug.Print(name + ": " + response.Headers[name]);
    }

    // response body
    var buffer = new byte[response.ContentLength];
    Stream stream = response.GetResponseStream();
    int toRead = buffer.Length;
    while (toRead > 0)
    {
        // already read: buffer.Length - toRead
        int read = stream.Read(buffer, buffer.Length - toRead,
            toRead);
        toRead = toRead - read;
    }
    char[] chars = Encoding.UTF8.GetChars(buffer);
    Debug.Print(new string(chars));
}
}
```

This example sends a GET request that fetches the most recent samples of all data streams of the given feed. The output written to the debug console—which is a reconstruction of the received HTTP response—may look like this:

```
HTTP/1.1 200 OK
Date: Thu, 24 Mar 2011 14:28:07 GMT
Content-Type: text/plain; charset=utf-8
Connection: keep-alive
Last-Modified: Thu, 24 Mar 2011 12:56:58 GMT
Content-Length: 67
Age: 0
Vary: Accept-Encoding
voltage,2011-03-24T12:56:58.990932Z,0.00
number,2011-03-23T16:03:03.461085Z,42
```

Note that a timestamp was added between the data stream ID and the sample's value. This is the time when the Pachube service received the sample.

# 8/Sending HTTP Requests—The Efficient Way

While the `HttpWebRequest` and `HttpWebResponse` classes are relatively convenient to use, they gobble up a large part of the available Flash and RAM on a Netduino Plus. Because they are built on top of the so-called *Socket API*, it can make sense to use the `Socket` API directly instead. This is more work, but it can reduce the *memory footprint* of an application considerably.

Moreover, the main message of this book is that HTTP is not black magic and requires neither high-powered computers nor huge, complex web frameworks. Using the `Socket` API makes that obvious, because you see much more of what really goes on than if you use only higher-level APIs. For this reason, I will show an alternative to `SimplePutRequest` called `EfficientPutRequest`—which is efficient mainly in the sense that it has a small memory footprint.

## EfficientPutRequest

To send a sample to Pachube, you can use the code in Example 8-1.

### Example 8-1. EfficientPutRequest

```
using System.Net;
using System.Net.Sockets;
using System.Text;
using Microsoft.SPOT;

public class EfficientPutRequest
```

```
{
    public static void Main()
    {
        const string apiKey = "your Pachube API key";
        const string feedId = "your Pachube feed id";

        // this is the "sample" we want to send to Pachube
        var sample = "number,43";
        // convert sample to byte array
        byte[] contentBuffer = Encoding.UTF8.GetBytes(sample);

        // produce request
        using (Socket connection = Connect("api.pachube.com", 5000))
        {
            SendRequest(connection, apiKey, feedId, sample);
        }
    }

    static Socket Connect(string host, int timeout)
    {
        // look up host's domain name to find IP address(es)
        IPHostEntry hostEntry = Dns.GetHostEntry(host);
        // extract a returned address
        IPAddress hostAddress = hostEntry.AddressList[0];
        IPEndPoint remoteEndPoint = new IPEndPoint(hostAddress, 80);

        // connect!
        Debug.Print("connect...");
        var connection = new Socket(AddressFamily.InterNetwork,
            SocketType.Stream, ProtocolType.Tcp);
        connection.Connect(remoteEndPoint);
        connection.SetSocketOption(SocketOptionLevel.Tcp,
            SocketOptionName.NoDelay, true);
        connection.SendTimeout = timeout;
        return connection;
    }

    static void SendRequest(Socket s, string apiKey, string feedId,
        string content)
    {
        byte[] contentBuffer = Encoding.UTF8.GetBytes(content);
        const string CRLF = "\r\n";
```

```
var requestLine =
    "PUT /v2/feeds/" + feedId + ".csv HTTP/1.1" + CRLF;
byte[] requestLineBuffer = Encoding.UTF8.
    GetBytes(requestLine);
var headers =
    "Host: api.pachube.com" + CRLF +
    "X-PachubeApiKey: " + apiKey + CRLF +
    "Content-Type: text/csv" + CRLF +
    "Content-Length: " + contentBuffer.Length + CRLF +
    CRLF;
byte[] headersBuffer = Encoding.UTF8.GetBytes(headers);
s.Send(requestLineBuffer);
s.Send(headersBuffer);
s.Send(contentBuffer);
    }
}
```

This example starts in the same way as `SimplePutRequest` (Example 7-1) from Chapter 7—with the two constants *apiKey* and *feedId*, which you must set to your API key and feed ID. Next, it opens a connection using the helper method `Connect`, and then it uses the helper method `SendRequest` to create the HTTP message and send it over the connection.

## The Connect Method

In the `Socket` API, a connection is represented as an instance of class `Socket`. When you create a socket with `new Socket()`, you pass several arguments required for the TCP/IP protocol. Then, you call the socket's `Connect` method with an `IPEndPoint` as an argument. This endpoint indicates the Internet address of Pachube and the port (80, which is the default port used by web servers) to which you want to send the request.

To get Pachube's Internet address, you first need to perform a DNS lookup, which is done in the `Dns.GetHostEntry` method. A timeout is set to make sure that the program does not get stuck waiting (*blocking*) forever, even if the network connection to Pachube, or Pachube itself, goes down for some reason.

Either the response arrives before this timeout elapses (great!), or the program continues without waiting any longer for the response (not great, but it's better than waiting forever).

# The SendRequest Method

A socket represents a two-way connection between client and server. The server waits until it receives a request message from the client. An HTTP request message consists of a request line, one or more header lines, an empty line, and then the optional message body (i.e., the actual content). Each line is terminated by a carriage return, followed by a line feed. For an example request, see the section "What Netduino Said to Pachube" in Chapter 6.

The request line contains the HTTP method, in this case a PUT, plus the request URI and the HTTP version (HTTP/1.1). For Pachube, new measurements are sent to the URI `http://api.pachube.com/v2/feeds/` `feedId.csv`. Only the relative path `/v2/feeds/feedId.csv` is used in the request line. It is spliced together out of its individual parts, of which the `feedId` is specific to your application.

---

NOTE: If your program constructs URIs in this fashion, make sure that it is easy to find all places in the program where you do this. Otherwise, maintenance can become very cumbersome—e.g., if the server's resource design changes, or if the client should be modified for an entirely different server.

---

The host part of the URI is given in the `Host` header. The content type and length (in bytes) are given in the `Content-Type` and `Content-Length` headers, respectively. You must also provide the Pachube-specific `X-PachubeApiKey` header, since the API key is used to make sure that you are authorized to send new samples to Pachube.

---

NOTE: Well, relatively sure, since the API key is sent in plain text over the network, making it available to snoopers. If you think your API key has been compromised, you can regenerate it by visiting the Pachube website, going to "my settings", and clicking Regenerate API Key. But if you do this, you'll have to modify all your existing programs to use the new API key.

---

Next, `SendRequest` converts the three parts of the request into byte arrays and sends them to Pachube over the socket.

Note that you now have a very good idea about what exactly goes over the wire. There is no longer a "magic" API that somehow produces or consumes the raw bytes. This is good to know, even if you choose to use a higher-level API in most cases. And more important, you've saved some precious memory on your Netduino Plus.

## How Can I Get the Response from Pachube?

Unlike `SimplePutRequest`, `EfficientPutRequest` ignores the response message coming back from Pachube; it operates purely in "fire and forget" mode. It is quite cumbersome to interpret an HTTP response message when using the `Socket` API. The reason is that when you start reading the bytes of the response message, it is not immediately clear where the message body starts, how long the message body is, or where exactly the information about the message body's length can be found.

It is clear, however, where the three bytes of the status code can be found:

```
HTTP/1.1 200 OK\r\n
```

Given this information, you could add a method `ReceiveResponse`, as given in Example 8-2.

## Example 8-2. ReceiveResponse

```
static void ReceiveResponse(Socket s)
{
    // status code is at positions 9 to 11, e.g.,
    // "HTTP/1.1 200..."
    var buffer = new byte[12];
    var i = 0;
    while (i != 12)
    {
        int read = s.Receive(buffer, i, 1, SocketFlags.None);
        i = i + 1;
    }
    const int zero = (int)'0';
    int statusCode =
        100 * (buffer[9] - zero) +
         10 * (buffer[10] - zero) +
             (buffer[11] - zero);
    Debug.Print("Response status code = " + statusCode);
}
```

This method reads exactly 12 bytes from the Pachube connection and then converts the last three bytes to an integer value. This is the status code value.

After sending the request, the response can now be received in this way within the `Main` method (the added line is shown in bold):

```
using (Socket connection = Connect("api.pachube.com", 5000))
{
    SendRequest(connection, apiKey, feedId, sample);
    ReceiveResponse(connection);
}
```

Unfortunately, it isn't that simple. When you try out this version of the client, you will get status code 200 (OK) for the first request. But the status codes for later requests will be nonsense. Try this out using the following modification:

```
// produce request
using (Socket connection = Connect("api.pachube.com", 5000))
{
    Debug.Print("sending first request");
    SendRequest(connection, apiKey, feedId, sample);
    ReceiveResponse(connection);

    Debug.Print("sending second request");
    SendRequest(connection, apiKey, feedId, sample);
    ReceiveResponse(connection);
}
```

The reason why the second response appears as garbage is that you have read (i.e., consumed) only the first 12 bytes of the first response. Remaining bytes of the status line, the headers, and the body will wait patiently until the client sends the second request and then calls `ReceiveResponse` again. Instead of receiving the status code for the second request, the client reads some garbage from the response to the first request.

To get rid of the old response, you would need to know precisely how long the response is and consume (receive) all remaining bytes—even if you are not interested in them. But since you don't know how long the response is, you'll have to resort to a brute force solution: close the connection after every request instead of keeping it open. In some cases, this approach will be sufficient; in others, you might prefer the simpler `HttpWebRequest` API as shown in Chapter 7.

# 9/Hello Pachube (Sockets Version)

In this chapter, I will present a version of a complete Pachube client that uses the `Socket` API. It demonstrates that this low-level API is a viable alternative, especially for "fire and forget" requests.

## PachubeClient

`HelloPachubeSockets` (Example 9-1) performs some initializations in its `Main` method, enters an endless loop in which it waits until it is time for the next measurement, performs the measurement, and then sends the result to Pachube. This is repeated every 20 seconds like in the original `HelloPachube` program.

### Example 9-1. HelloPachubeSockets

```
using System;
using System.Net;
using System.Net.Sockets;
using System.Text;
using System.Threading;
using Microsoft.SPOT;
using Microsoft.SPOT.Hardware;
using SecretLabs.NETMF.Hardware.NetduinoPlus;

public class HelloPachubeSockets
{
    public static void Main()
    {
        const string apiKey = "your Pachube API key";
        const string feedId = "your Pachube feed id";
        const int samplingPeriod = 20000;   // 20 seconds

        const double maxVoltage = 3.3;
```

```csharp
const int maxAdcValue = 1023;

var voltagePort = new AnalogInput(Pins.GPIO_PIN_A1);
var lowPort = new OutputPort(Pins.GPIO_PIN_A0, false);
var highPort = new OutputPort(Pins.GPIO_PIN_A2, true);

Socket connection = null;

while (true)    // main loop
{
    WaitUntilNextPeriod(samplingPeriod);

    Debug.Print("time: " + DateTime.Now);
    Debug.Print("memory available: " + Debug.GC(true));

    if (connection == null)    // create connection
    {
        try
        {
            connection = Connect("api.pachube.com",
                samplingPeriod / 2);
        }
        catch
        {
            Debug.Print("connection error");
        }
    }

    if (connection != null)
    {
        try
        {
            int rawValue = voltagePort.Read();
            double value = (rawValue * maxVoltage) /
                maxAdcValue;
            string sample = "voltage," + value.ToString("f");
            Debug.Print("new message: " + sample);
            SendRequest(connection, apiKey, feedId, sample);
        }
        catch (SocketException)
```

```
                {
                    connection.Close();
                    connection = null;
                }
            }
        }
    }

    static Socket Connect(string host, int timeout)
    {
        // look up host's domain name to find IP address(es)
        IPHostEntry hostEntry = Dns.GetHostEntry(host);
        // extract a returned address
        IPAddress hostAddress = hostEntry.AddressList[0];
        IPEndPoint remoteEndPoint = new IPEndPoint(hostAddress, 80);

        // connect!
        Debug.Print("connect...");
        var connection = new Socket(AddressFamily.InterNetwork,
            SocketType.Stream, ProtocolType.Tcp);
        connection.Connect(remoteEndPoint);
        connection.SetSocketOption(SocketOptionLevel.Tcp,
            SocketOptionName.NoDelay, true);
        connection.SendTimeout = timeout;
        return connection;
    }

    static void SendRequest(Socket s, string apiKey, string feedId,
        string content)
    {
        byte[] contentBuffer = Encoding.UTF8.GetBytes(content);
        const string CRLF = "\r\n";
        var requestLine =
            "PUT /v2/feeds/" + feedId + ".csv HTTP/1.1" + CRLF;
        byte[] requestLineBuffer = Encoding.UTF8.
            GetBytes(requestLine);
        var headers =
            "Host: api.pachube.com" + CRLF +
            "X-PachubeApiKey: " + apiKey + CRLF +
            "Content-Type: text/csv" + CRLF +
```

```
                "Content-Length: " + contentBuffer.Length + CRLF +
                CRLF;
            byte[] headersBuffer = Encoding.UTF8.GetBytes(headers);
            s.Send(requestLineBuffer);
            s.Send(headersBuffer);
            s.Send(contentBuffer);
        }


        static void WaitUntilNextPeriod(int period)
        {
            long now = DateTime.Now.Ticks / TimeSpan.TicksPerMillisecond;
            var offset = (int)(now % period);
            int delay = period - offset;
            Debug.Print("sleep for " + delay + " ms\r\n");
            Thread.Sleep(delay);
        }
    }
```

To run the program:

1. Create a new Visual Studio project (using the Netduino Plus template) and name it HelloPachubeSockets. Replace the contents of *Program.cs* with the code from Example 9-1.

2. Replace the strings for *apiKey* and *feedId* so they match your Pachube API key and feed ID.

3. Next, build the project and deploy it to your Netduino Plus, as described in the section "Deploying to the Device" in Chapter 1.


## Viewing the Results

When the Pachube client is started, something like the following output will be shown:

```
sleep for 6520 ms

time: 01/01/2009 00:00:20
memory available: 34656
connect...
new message: voltage,3.27
sleep for 9700 ms
```

```
time: 01/01/2009 01:10:20
memory available: 33120
new message: voltage,2.32
sleep for 9854 ms

time: 01/01/2009 01:10:30
memory available: 33120
new message: voltage,0.98
sleep for 9854 ms

...
```

Note the connect… message in the first iteration of the loop, and how the available memory decreases and then stabilizes after a few iterations.

## How It Works

The initializations in Main start with the same constants as in Hello-Pachube: *apiKey*, *feedId*, and samplingPeriod. This is followed by the same constants and variables as in HelloPachube.

What is new is the variable connection, which is initialized to null. It represents a TCP/IP connection to Pachube.

The main loop does basically three things:

1. It sleeps until the next sample is due, takes the sample, and then sends it to Pachube.

2. It uses the helper method WaitUntilNextPeriod, which we already know from Chapter 6.

3. It also uses the helper methods Connect and SendRequest, which we already know from Chapter 6.

Two Debug.Print statements give you information about when a sample is taken and how much memory is currently available for new objects.

To send an HTTP request to Pachube, a TCP/IP connection to Pachube must first be opened. Through the main loop, the example tries to establish such a connection if it doesn't already exist. When calling the helper method Connect to open a connection, a *timeout*, given in milliseconds, is passed as an argument. This is the time span after which the client stops waiting for a response—e.g., when the server is unavailable or there is a network problem between client and server. Here, I simply pass the sampling period divided by two, which gives this program a reasonable timeout period.

Creating a connection may fail, which the `Socket` API will report by throwing an exception. To make sure that the program continues even if such a (hopefully temporary) problem occurs, a `try/catch` statement is used to handle the exceptions. If an exception occurs, it is caught, and the message "connection error" is printed to the Output window.

---

NOTE: You should only try to handle exceptions for *expected errors*—i.e., for situations that may occur under normal operating conditions, such as errors in opening or using an Internet connection due to some network or server problems.

By contrast, exceptions that indicate *program errors* should not be handled. On the contrary, they should become apparent—and be corrected—as early as possible. For example, if you call:

```
Socket c = Connect(null, timeout)
```

instead of:

```
Socket c = Connect("api.pachube.com", timeout)
```

you will get an exception. It wouldn't make sense to catch such an exception and hope that an exception handler provides the correct host address in some magical way. Instead, an unhandled exception produces an error message that can give you a good idea of where there is a bug that needs to be corrected.

---

If a connection already existed or a new one was opened successfully, the example sends a request to Pachube containing the new sample. If an exception occurs when trying to send the request, the connection is closed. Otherwise, it is kept open, since opening a connection is an expensive operation (it takes up CPU time, which is in short supply on a small microcontroller).

# III/Device as HTTP Server

When you hear the term "server," you may think of an expensive high-performance machine somewhere in a data center. By contrast, you may think of a client as a modest PC, or even a lowly embedded device like the Netduino Plus. In fact, Figure III-1 is pretty representative of most Internet servers and clients today.

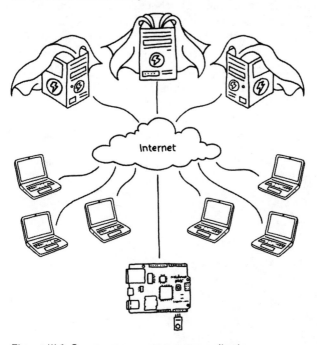

Figure III-1. Super servers versus puny clients

It's not only the processing power and storage that separates Internet clients and servers. There is another difference: an Internet server has a *unique static Internet address* that makes it "visible" from anywhere. A client has only a nonunique private Internet address and is "visible" only within a local network, e.g., your home network. A client can "dial out" to an Internet server, as you did with the Pachube clients, but no one can "dial in" to the device. Why not? Because your home router and the routers of your Internet provider have firewalls and perform network address translation in order to save Internet addresses. In some cases, you can circumvent this using a *port forwarding* mechanism in your router. Therefore, devices as servers seem to be reserved for corporations that can afford static Internet addresses, or for the lucky few with the right know-how, equipment, and Internet service providers. (Or perhaps for a time in the future when the entire Internet is able to handle IPv6 addresses and no network address translation is performed anymore.) However, as I will show in Chapter 10, there is now a simple way to turn even a Netduino Plus into a true Internet server, and thereby into a first-class citizen of the Internet.

A device as client is often an appropriate choice; we have seen examples where a Netduino Plus sends samples to Pachube for further processing, storage, visualization, etc. However, you may not only want to *observe* the physical world, but also to *influence* it. For example, you may want to turn on the heat in your mountain cabin before you visit it. Or you may want to allow your friends to register an HTTP message at your device that will be sent to them when the mountain cabin has become invitingly warm. Or perhaps you want Pachube to monitor the warmth of the cabin and switch off the heat when it reaches a particular temperature. And so on. Such scenarios would greatly benefit if devices can be programmed as servers.

If devices remained limited to clients, they would create a rather narrow and uninspiring form of the Internet of Things. This part of the book shows how you can venture beyond that.

# 10/Hello Web

On the Web, the equivalent to HelloWorld is a server program that handles GET requests from web browsers and returns a message to them, as shown in Figure 10-1.

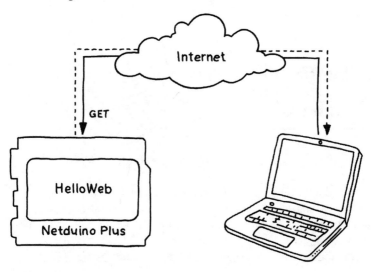

*Figure 10-1. Architecture of HelloWeb*

## Relaying Messages to and from the Netduino

Isn't there supposed to be a problem with making a device a web server, as mentioned in Part III? How can we sidestep the problems caused by firewalls, network address translations, and the shortage of IPv4 Internet addresses?

The HelloWeb program works thanks to a *relay* between the Netduino Plus and the client who wants to connect to it over the Internet. The client sends its request not directly to the device, but instead to this relay; from there, the request is forwarded to the device. The response comes back the same way, indirectly, via the relay (see Figure 10-2).

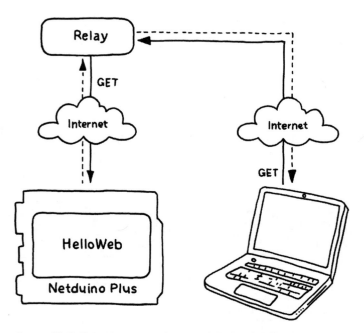

*Figure 10-2. Relay between client and device (application view)*

You may wonder how that setup solves any problem. After all, the device (your Netduino Plus) is still buried behind a NAT and firewall, and it therefore has no unique public Internet address to which requests could be sent. A client can obviously send requests to the *relay*, but how can the relay forward it to the device if the device cannot even be addressed?

The relay solves this problem because it allows us to cheat: from the application's point of view, the device indeed receives requests that come from somewhere on the Web. Under the hood, however, the device is actually an HTTP *client* that registers itself at the relay and keeps an open TCP/IP connection to the relay. When the relay receives a request from a client, it forwards it to the device over the open connection, receives the device's response, and sends it back to the client. The client therefore never needs to "see" the device directly; it uses a URI pointing to the relay instead.

Since requests and responses travel "the wrong way" between device and relay, this approach is sometimes called *reverse HTTP*. There are several ways in which a reverse HTTP protocol can be defined—the important point is that it is possible to create a relay without running afoul of the rules of the HTTP protocol.

## Yaler

My company, Oberon microsystems, developed a reverse HTTP relay called *Yaler* (relay spelled backwards) because several of our customers needed a robust and scalable relay for their devices. The source code for Yaler is available at *http://yaler.org/*. If you have a Windows or Linux server with a public Internet address, you can set up your own relay by downloading and running Yaler.

For the time being, a hosted Yaler instance is set up specifically for readers of *Getting Started with the Internet of Things* at *http://try.yaler.net/*. It is free for personal and educational use, and is without service or uptime guarantees. In the future, yaler.net might become a commercial, hosted service. It requires an authorization key similar to a Pachube API key. Please see *http://www.gsiot.info/yaler* for up-to-date information on how to get your secret key, as well as a *relay domain* for your device (this is a unique identifier for your device, similar to a Pachube feed ID).

# HelloWeb

Example 10-1 shows `HelloWeb`, our first web server program using a relay. Note that the relay domain and secret key used below are just examples that won't work for you, so you need to provide your own values. Alternatively, if you only want to try out the server within your home network, you can just omit the `RelayDomain` and `RelaySecretKey` lines completely (or comment out by prefixing them with //), thereby switching off the relay mechanism.

## Example 10-1. HelloWeb

```
using Gsiot.Server;

public class HelloWeb
{
    public static void Main()
    {
        var webServer = new HttpServer
        {
            RelayDomain = "gsiot-FFMQ-TTD5",
            RelaySecretKey =
                "o5fIIZS5tpD2A4Zp87CoKNUsSpIEJZrV5rNjpg89",
            RequestRouting =
```

```
        {
            {
                "GET /hello",
                context =>
                  { context.SetResponse("Hello Web",
                      "text/plain"); }
            }
        }
    };
    webServer.Run();
  }
}
```

To build and run the program, perform the following steps:

1. Make sure that your Netduino Plus is connected to your Ethernet router and that it is correctly configured for network access. If the Pachube client examples from Part II work, you are all set.

2. If you haven't done so yet, download the Visual Studio project Gsiot.Server from *http://www.gsiot.info/download/*, unzip it, and put it into the *Visual Studio 2010\Projects\* directory.

3. Create a new Visual Studio project (using the Netduino Plus template) and name it HelloWeb. Replace the contents of *Program.cs* with the code from Example 10-1.

4. Obtain your own relay domain and secret relay key by following the instructions on *http://www.gsiot.info/yaler*.

5. Assign your device's relay domain to variable `RelayDomain`.

6. Assign your secret relay key to variable `RelaySecretKey`.

7. Right-click on References in the Solution Explorer. Select Add→ New Reference.... In the Add Reference dialog box, click on the Browse tab. In the directory hierarchy, go up two levels to the *Project* directory. In the *Gsiot.Server* directory, open the *Gsiot.Server* subdirectory (yes, the same name again). In this directory, open the

*bin* subdirectory. From there, open the *Release* subdirectory. In this directory, select the *Gsiot.Server.dll* file. Click the OK button. You have now added the assembly *Projects\Gsiot.Server\Gsiot.Server\bin\ Release\Gsiot.Server.dll*.

8. Next, build the project and deploy it to your Netduino Plus, as described in the section "Deploying to the Device" in Chapter 1.

## Viewing the Results

On the debug console, a typical output of HelloWeb may look like this:

```
DHCP enabled: True
MAC address: 3C-8A-4A-00-00-07
Device address: 192.168.5.100
Gateway address: 192.168.5.11
Primary DNS address: 192.168.5.11
Base URI: http://try.yaler.net/gsiot-FFMQ-TTD5/
```

Open your favorite web browser and enter the above *base URI* for accessing your Netduino Plus. When you send a request with a URI that starts with this base URI, it will be sent via the relay to your device.

When you enter the URI in your program, be sure to change *gsiot-FFMQ-TTD5* to your relay domain.

Something like the following output should be printed to the debug console:

```
memory available: 11424
GET /gsiot-FFMQ-TTD5/hello -> 200
```

When you look at your browser window, it should show a web page with the string:

```
Hello Web
```

Congratulations! Your first server program is up and running, accessible from any corner of the earth!

# Using C# Initializers to Create the HttpServer

The `HelloWeb` program from Example 10-1 executes two statements in its `Main` method. The first statement creates an `HttpServer` object and stores it in the variable `webServer`. The second statement starts this server by calling its `Run` method.

We can use the C# initializer syntax to create an `HttpServer` object and initialize all its key values in one go:

```
var webServer = new HttpServer
{
    RelayDomain = …,
    RelaySecretKey = …,
    RequestRouting = …
};
```

An initializer is a sequence of property or field initializations enclosed in curly braces after new *SomeClassName*. Individual initializations are separated by commas. Such initializers are a convenience feature that can make code more readable, particularly if a large number of properties are involved. The above example is equivalent to:

```
var webServer = new HttpServer();
webServer.RelayDomain = …;
webServer.RelaySecretKey = …;
webServer.RequestRouting = …;
```

The individual initializations have the form:

```
Field = Expression
```

Initializers can also be used to initialize the elements of a *collection*, as in this example:

```
RequestRouting =
{
    { "GET /hello", HandleGetHello },
    { "GET /about.html", HandleGetAboutHtml }
}
```

The C# compiler translates this into the following:

```
RequestRouting.Add("GET /hello", HandleGetHello);
RequestRouting.Add("GET /about.html", HandleGetAboutHtml);
```

## C#'s Lambda Expression Shorthand

You may have wondered about the following expression in Example 10-1:

```
context => { context.SetResponse("Hello Web", "text/plain"); }
```

This is an example of a C# *lambda expression*. A lambda expression uses the *lambda operator* => (i.e., "goes to"):

» On its left side, there are zero, one, or more input parameters; in this example, there is one parameter: `context`.

» On its right side, between curly braces, there is a statement that can use the input parameter.

In this case, `context` is of type `RequestHandlerContext`. This type has a method `SetResponse`; the lambda expression sets the HTTP response message body to `Hello Web`, and the response message header `Content-Type` to `text/plain` (and, implicitly, the response message's status code to 200, i.e., OK).

Lambda expressions are a shorthand way of writing down what would otherwise be a complete method.[1] For example, the compiler performs the necessary calculations to determine the type of `context`. Written in traditional form, the above example would look like this:

```
static void HandleGetHello(RequestHandlerContext context)
{
    context.SetResponse("Hello Web", "text/plain");
}
```

---

[1] I use lambda expressions for single statements, but I usually prefer complete methods for longer blocks of code.

# Request Handlers

The web server's `RequestRouting` property is used to specify which *request handler* will handle which request pattern (request methods such as GET, request URIs such as `/hello`).

For example, the pair:

```
{ "GET /hello", HandleGetHello }
```

declares that when a GET request with the request URI `/hello` has been received, the method `HandleGetHello` should be called for handling this request.

The *request pattern* string, e.g., `"GET /hello"`, first gives the HTTP method that is accepted—in this case, GET. This is followed by a blank, which is followed by the request URI: a relative URI that starts with a `/` character. If your request handler can support several HTTP methods, you can pass the `*` character instead of an HTTP method name, e.g., `"* /led/target"`. If your request handler is able to support several resources with the same URI prefix, you can pass a `*` character at the end, e.g., `"GET /sensors/*"`.

A request handler has a *context* object of type `RequestHandlerContext` as a parameter. This object contains the necessary information about the HTTP request, an empty representation of the HTTP response to be sent (which you'll fill in with a content type and response text before the response is sent back), and some information related to the server—e.g., the base URI of the server. It has the following interface:

```
public class RequestHandlerContext
{
    public RequestHandlerContext(string serviceRoot,
        string relayDomain);
    public bool ConnectionClose { get; set; }

    // request interface
    public string RequestMethod { get; }
    public string RequestUri { get; }
    public string RequestContentType { get; }
    public string RequestContent { get; }
```

```
// server interface
public string BuildRequestUri(string path);
public string BuildAbsoluteRequestUri(string path);

// response interface
public int ResponseStatusCode { get; set; }
public string ResponseContentType { get; set; }
public string ResponseContent { get; set; }
public void SetResponse(string content, string textType);
}
```

This interface is described in more detail in Appendix C. Here, the most
important thing you should know is that a **RequestHandlerContext**
object provides the property **ResponseStatusCode** that you can set to
return a response message without a message body, and a method
**SetResponse** that you can call to set the response status code to 200
(OK), to set the **Content-Type** HTTP header, and to set the message
body to some string (**content**). (The **Content-Length** property is always
calculated automatically.)

# HelloWebHtml

Let's now look at a slightly more interesting version of **HelloWeb**.
**HelloWebHtml** (Example 10-2) returns an HTML representation. The
word **Web** is printed in bold using HTML's **strong** element. In addition,
**HelloWebHtml** adds the time that has passed since the Netduino Plus
was last booted, so you can check more easily whether the server is
running. If you refresh the web page and the time display changes, the
server still runs fine.

## Example 10-2. HelloWebHtml

```
using System;
using Gsiot.Server;

public class HelloWebHtml
{
    public static void Main()
    {
        var webServer = new HttpServer
```

```
        {
            RelayDomain = "gsiot-FFMQ-TTD5",
            RelaySecretKey =
                "o5fIIZS5tpD2A4Zp87CoKNUsSpIEJZrV5rNjpg89",
            RequestRouting =
            {
                { "GET /hello.html", HandleGetHelloHtml }
            }
        };
        webServer.Run();
    }

    static void HandleGetHelloHtml(RequestHandlerContext context)
    {
        string s =
            "<html>\r\n" +
            "\t<body>\r\n" +
            "\t\tHello <strong>Web</strong> at " +
                DateTime.Now + "\r\n" +
            "\t</body>\r\n" +
            "</html>";
        context.SetResponse(s, "text/html");
    }
}
```

A web page created by `HelloWebHtml` might look like this:

```
Hello Web at 01/01/2009 00:01:11
```

As you can see, an HTTP server doesn't need to be a complicated beast!

# What You Should Know About Ports

An HTTP server indicates its readiness to receive HTTP requests by "listening" on a *port*. By convention, port 80 is used for the HTTP protocol. Other Internet protocols use different ports; the port numbers between 1 and 49151 are reserved for use by standard protocols. On many operating systems, ports up to 1000 require special privileges. On your Netduino Plus, there are no such restrictions.

---

NOTE: The use of ports in this way is merely a convention. Nothing prevents you from using one of the reserved ports for your own server programs, as long as no other program is already listening on that port. I often use port 8080 during development, which also works on a PC.

---

If you have used http://192.168.5.100/*some-resource* as a URI in your web browser, the browser sends a GET request to the program that listens on port 80 of device 192.168.5.100. If no device with this Internet address is found, or no program on this device is currently listening on port 80, your web browser will show an error message—e.g., "Internet Explorer cannot display the webpage" in Internet Explorer, or "Address Not Found" in Firefox.

Because we use a relay in our server examples, the Netduino Plus is not really an HTTP server, and it therefore needs no port to listen for requests. If you only want to use your device as a server within your local area network, or if you use port forwarding instead of a relay, you can disable the relay mechanism by deleting these two property initializations:

```
RelayDomain = …,
RelaySecretKey = …,
```

Then, the Netduino Plus acts as a normal HTTP server. By default, it listens on port 80. If you want to use another port, set up the optional Port property, like this:

```
var webServer = new HttpServer
{
    Port = 8080,
    RequestRouting =
    {
        {
            "GET /hello",
            context =>
                { context.SetResponse("Hello Web", "text/plain"); }
        }
    }
};
```

This possibility can come in handy for testing purposes because it functions even if the Internet connection or the relay doesn't work for some reason. You can then test whether the server at least works within your home network.

## Port Forwarding

*Port forwarding* is a mechanism in your router that makes the service running on your Netduino Plus look to the Internet at large to implement the router itself. Therefore, the *router's* Internet address will be the Internet address of the services—not the private Internet address of your board. One problem with this setting is that the router's Internet address is dynamically assigned by your Internet provider, so it may change at any time. Usually it does not change often, but you cannot assume that it *never* changes. If a client program uses such a dynamic Internet address, the client must be updated after an address change—of which both your server program and the client(s) are unaware. You can alleviate this problem by using a dynamic DNS service to give your computer a host name that remains stable, even if the IP address of your router changes. One example is the free service of DynDNS.com (*http://www.dyndns.com/services/dns/dyndns/*).

As you can see, port forwarding requires a fair amount of network know-how. It works differently on different brands of routers that support it, may require firewall configuration changes, and only works with some Internet providers.

# 11/Handling Sensor Requests

`HelloWeb` (see Chapter 10) is an example of an HTTP server, but it doesn't use any sensors or actuators. In this chapter, I'll show how you can add sensor access to your server programs (Figure 11-1).

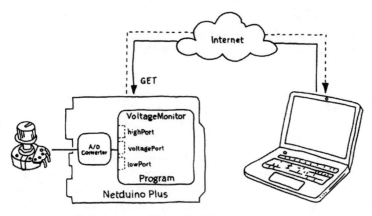

*Figure 11-1. Architecture of VoltageMonitor*

`VoltageMonitor`, which you'll see later in Example 11-1, shows how to handle GET requests to a sensor resource, more specifically one that represents some voltage—e.g., a voltage produced by an attached potentiometer, photo resistor, or similar sensor. You can use any web browser as a client to inspect the current voltage. After all, a web browser is basically an engine for initiating GET requests—and for displaying the responses, of course.

# From Sensor Readings to HTTP Resources

An HTTP server manages *resources*. In this example, a resource is provided that has the meaning, "actual voltage value, as measured by a sensor attached to the board." A resource that contains an *actual value* is called a *measured variable*. A measured variable changes its value over time, depending on a physical process: when the user physically turns the potentiometer's knob, the measured variable changes its value accordingly. This means that subsequent GET requests to the same resource may yield different responses.

A resource for a measured variable should reflect a physical phenomenon as it currently is. The resource is updated with new sensor values from time to time. Only GET requests are supported for measured variable resources.

When your server starts up, you'll typically create objects in your code that represent the value of these measured variables.

-----------------------------------------------------------------------

NOTE: "Measured variable," like "manipulated variable" (see Chapter 12), is a *process control* term (*http://www.wisc-online.com/objects/ViewObject.aspx?ID=IAU3306*). Process control is a discipline that deals with how to keep a physical process under control, e.g., keeping a boat on track even if there are currents and side winds.

-----------------------------------------------------------------------

# URIs of Measured Variables

How a request URI for a measured variable looks is entirely up to you. By convention, I will call measured variables */name/actual*—in this case, **/voltage/actual**. However, you can use any URI as long as you use only ASCII letters, digits, and the characters /, ?, #, [, ], @, !, $, &, ', (, ), *, +, ,, ;, and =. For example, the relative URI **/root/sensors/analog/1** would be a perfectly legitimate alternative and would look like this:

```
http://192.168.5.100/root/sensors/analog/1
```

---

NOTE: Just because you set up your server to reply to a request with a long request URI doesn't mean you have to support resources for such URIs as the following, which exist all along the path:

```
http://192.168.5.100/root/sensors/analog
```

```
http://192.168.5.100/root/sensors
```

```
http://192.168.5.100/root
```

```
http://192.168.5.100/
```

---

# VoltageMonitor

`VoltageMonitor`, shown in Example 11-1, supports GET requests for a measured variable resource. One resource is supported: an ASCII representation of the current value of the voltage produced by the attached potentiometer.

## Example 11-1. VoltageMonitor

```
using Gsiot.Server;
using Microsoft.SPOT.Hardware;
using SecretLabs.NETMF.Hardware.NetduinoPlus;

public class VoltageMonitor
{
    public static void Main()
    {
        // ground and power for the potentiometer
        var lowPort = new OutputPort(Pins.GPIO_PIN_A0, false);
        var highPort = new OutputPort(Pins.GPIO_PIN_A2, true);

        var voltageSensor = new AnalogSensor
        {
            InputPin = Pins.GPIO_PIN_A1,
            MinValue = 0.0,
            MaxValue = 3.3
        };

        var webServer = new HttpServer
        {
            RelayDomain = "gsiot-FFMQ-TTD5",
```

```
        RelaySecretKey =
            "o5fIIZS5tpD2A4Zp87CoKNUsSpIEJZrV5rNjpg89",
        RequestRouting =
        {
            {
                "GET /voltage/actual",
                new MeasuredVariable
                {
                    FromSensor = voltageSensor.HandleGet
                }.HandleRequest
            }
        }
    };

        webServer.Run();
    }
}
```

---

NOTE: To build and run this example, follow the steps in the section "HelloWeb" in Chapter 10, but name the project VoltageMonitor instead of HelloWeb.

---

To provide power and ground to the attached potentiometer, I use the same pins as in Chapter 3, configured as digital outputs, i.e., **A0** and **A2**.

For reading the current voltage, I use a library class **AnalogSensor** that wraps an analog input port (see Chapter 3) in an object that provides the method **HandleGet**. This method reads the input port and returns the result. Variable **voltageSensor** is an instance of **AnalogSensor**, initialized with pin **A1**. Moreover, properties **MinValue** and **MaxValue** make it possible for the analog sensor object to convert the integer input of the analog input port to a value in the given range—in this case, between 0.0 and 3.3.

In the **webServer** initialization, I use the request handler **HandleRequest** provided by an object of type **MeasuredVariable**. A **MeasuredVariable** object has a property **FromSensor**.

When a client makes a GET request for **/voltage/actual**, the request is passed to **MeasuredVariable**'s **HandleRequest** method. When this happens, the **MeasuredVariable** object first calls **FromSensor** in order to obtain a new sample. It then converts this sample to a string; after, it sends this string to the client as its response message body.

## Treating Variables Like Methods with C# Delegates

FromSensor is a property to which you can assign a method—i.e., a C# *delegate* property. Delegate properties must be compatible with the delegate types they represent.

For example, FromSensor must be compatible with the delegate type GetHandler, which was declared inside of Gsiot.Server:

```
delegate object GetHandler();
```

This is the case for AnalogSensor.HandleGet, so we can set the property FromSensor to voltageSensor.HandleGet. This allows webServer to interact with the voltageSensor's HandleGet method.

---

NOTE: Where is voltageSensor's HandleGet method? All you've seen so far is its declaration and initialization:

```
var voltageSensor = new AnalogSensor
{
    InputPin = Pins.GPIO_PIN_A1,
    MinValue = 0.0,
    MaxValue = 3.3
};
```

The voltageSensor's HandleGet method resides in the class definition of AnalogSensor, which you'll see in the next section.

---

If you think of normal methods as "method constants," then delegates are "method variables." In other words, you can assign methods to delegate variables and pass them around before calling them.

This indirect approach to calling a method allows the MeasureVariable object to be completely oblivious of the exact method that it calls. It simply assumes that a delegate property has been initialized with some suitable method. The compiler makes sure that at least the parameters and return type are correct.

NOTE: For a method to be compatible with a delegate property, the name
of the method and the parameter names are not relevant, nor is whether
the method is declared as static or not.

## Inside Gsiot.Server's AnalogSensor Class

The library class AnalogSensor is implemented in namespace Gsiot.Server,
as shown in Example 11-2. You don't need to include this code in your project
since it's already inside of Gsiot.Server.

## Example 11-2. AnalogSensor

```
public class AnalogSensor
{
    const int maxAdcValue = 1023;              // for 10-bit resolution

    public Cpu.Pin InputPin { get; set; }
    AnalogInput port;

    public double MinValue { get; set; }
    public double MaxValue { get; set; }
    double Delta;

    public void Open()
    {
        port = new AnalogInput(InputPin);
        Delta = MaxValue - MinValue;
    }

    public object HandleGet()
    {
        if (port == null) { Open(); }
        int rawValue = port.Read();
        return MinValue + ((rawValue * Delta) / maxAdcValue);
    }
}
```

The purpose of this class is to provide a common interface for sensors—namely, a method that produces new samples and is compatible with the delegate type GetHandler, and with a "declarative" initialization mechanism like the one of HttpServer.

## Inside Gsiot.Server's MeasuredVariable Class

The library class MeasuredVariable is implemented in namespace Gsiot.Server in the following way (see Example 11-3).

### Example 11-3. MeasuredVariable

```
public class MeasuredVariable
{
    public GetHandler FromSensor { get; set; }

    public void HandleRequest(RequestHandlerContext context)
    {
        object sample = FromSensor();
        // sample may be null
        CSharpRepresentation.Serialize(context, sample);
    }
}
```

The purpose of this request handler for measured variables is to separate the request processing from the way new samples are produced (FromSensor).

# What You Should Know About HTTP GET

To query the state of a device's sensor, send it HTTP GET messages. GET is defined as harmless in that it leaves no trace on the resources it accesses. Therefore, your server must not change any of its resources as a side effect of responding to a GET request. The only state changes due to a GET request should be for monitoring purposes—e.g., to keep track of how many GET requests have been handled since the server was started.

As a consequence, you should never use GET for changing a resource, starting an activity, or producing another side effect. So you shouldn't put links into your web pages that, when clicked, cause the formatting of a hard disk, the firing of a rocket, the closing of a valve, etc. If you want to do that from a web page, include buttons and JavaScript scripts to send the appropriate requests (e.g., PUT requests). This will be shown in Chapter 12.

HTTP GET is sometimes called *idempotent*, which in computer science is a term that refers to an operation that produces the same result even if you apply it more than once. In this context, it means that issuing the same GET request successively multiple times has the same effect on the server's resources as issuing it only once. This is trivially established, since a GET request should have *no* effect on the server's resources.

The term is misleading, however, in that the same GET request sent multiple times to the same host does *not* necessarily return the same response every time. This is obvious for measured variables: a GET request provides the most recent measurement of a physical process that is changing continuously.

# 12/Handling Actuator Requests

To change the state of a resource, a web client can send PUT requests. A PUT request contains a representation of the desired new state of the resource. In this chapter's example, an LED's state (on/off) is controlled through a web service, as illustrated in Figure 12-1.

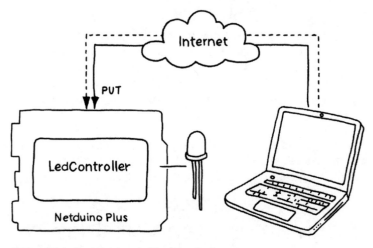

*Figure 12-1. Architecture of LedController*

LedController shows how to handle PUT requests; thus, it is a server program. Unfortunately, you cannot directly use a web browser as a client for sending PUT requests because web browsers are focused on GET requests. Later in this chapter you will see how you can write your own client program (in both C# and JavaScript versions) for testing the server.

------------------------------------------------------------

NOTE: If you don't mind learning your way around tools like cURL (*http://curl.haxx.se/docs/*) or the Poster add-on for Firefox (*https://addons.mozilla.org/en-US/firefox/addon/poster/*), you can initiate PUT requests with these as well.

For example, with the cURL command-line utility—which is usually installed by default on Mac OS X and Linux—you could use a command like this to turn the LED on (be sure to change the URI to match your configuration):

```
curl -X PUT -d true \

  http://try.yaler.net/gsiot-FFMQ-TTD5/led/target
```

---

# From HTTP Resources to Controlling Things

The resource managed in this example has the meaning "desired state of the LED on the board." Such a resource that accepts *target values* (or *setpoints*) is called a *manipulated variable*. When a server receives a PUT request for a manipulated variable resource, it takes the setpoint value contained in the request message body and feeds it to an actuator. In this example, the actuator is simply an LED.

A server that supports a manipulated variable may or may not support GET requests, in addition to PUT requests, for this resource. A GET request may simply return the most recent PUT value.

# URIs of Manipulated Variables

By convention, manipulated variables in this book are called /*name*/target; in this case /led/target:

```
  http://192.168.5.100/led/target
```

In more complicated applications than this example here, it may not be certain that putting a target value will really have the desired physical effect. For example, if you send a PUT request to a manipulated variable for a valve, with "closed" as the desired state, there may be mechanical reasons why this desired state is not achieved (e.g., the valve may have become mechanically blocked). In such situations, it might make sense to additionally provide a measured variable (sensor) for the valve. This would result in two separate resources: one for the actuator and one for the sensor:

```
http://192.168.5.100/valve/target
http://192.168.5.100/valve/actual
```

The distinction between these two resources reflects the physical reality of a device that has both a sensor (producing the actual value) and an actuator (changing state based on the target value). You may also provide a more abstract combined resource. For example, "state of the fountain in my garden" returns the actual value of the fountain's valve in response to a GET request, and accepts a target value for the valve as part of a PUT request:

```
http://192.168.5.100/fountain-state
```

You can play with the resources until you find the most suitable design for your application. People like different ways to "see" into a system. For example, your parents may only be interested in a temperature given in degrees Celsius, whereas you may be interested in the raw values returned by the sensor—especially if your parents complain that the temperature values cannot be correct. Maybe the sensor is defective, or the algorithm that translates raw sensor values to human-readable engineering units is buggy. Then, it helps to provide both the raw value and the processed value as resources.

# LedController

The structure of `LedController` (Example 12-1) is very similar to that of Example 11-1, `VoltageMonitor`.

## Example 12-1. LedController

```
using Gsiot.Server;
using SecretLabs.NETMF.Hardware.NetduinoPlus;

public class LedController
{
    public static void Main()
    {
        var ledActuator = new DigitalActuator
```

```
    {
        OutputPin = Pins.ONBOARD_LED
    };

    var webServer = new HttpServer
    {
        RelayDomain = "gsiot-FFMQ-TTD5",
        RelaySecretKey =
            "o5fIIZS5tpD2A4Zp87CoKNUsSpIEJZrV5rNjpg89",
        RequestRouting =
        {
            {
                "PUT /led/target",
                new ManipulatedVariable
                {
                    FromHttpRequest =
                        CSharpRepresentation.TryDeserializeBool,
                    ToActuator = ledActuator.HandlePut
                }.HandleRequest
            }
        }
    };

    webServer.Run();
    }
}
```

The main differences between the two examples are that Example 12-1 uses an instance of DigitalActuator (ledActuator) instead of Analog-Sensor, and an instance of ManipulatedVariable (created using C#'s initializer syntax that was explained in Chapter 10) instead of Measured-Variable.

A ManipulatedVariable instance has a delegate property FromHttpRequest for the conversion from an HTTP message body to a setpoint object, and a ToActuator delegate property for applying the setpoint to an actuator.

FromHttpRequest must be compatible with this delegate type:

```
delegate bool Deserializer(RequestHandlerContext context,
    out object content);
```

and ToActuator must be compatible with this delegate type:

```
delegate void PutHandler(object o);
```

Library method CSharpRepresentation.TryDeserializeBool is compatible with Deserializer, so it can be assigned to ToHttpResponse. The method ledActuator.HandlePut is compatible with PutHandler, so it can be assigned to ToActuator.

## Inside Gsiot.Server's DigitalActuator Class

The library class DigitalActuator is implemented in namespace Gsiot. Server, as shown in Example 12-2.

## Example 12-2. DigitalActuator

```
public class DigitalActuator
{
    public Cpu.Pin OutputPin { get; set; }

    OutputPort port;

    public void Open()
    {
        port = new OutputPort(OutputPin, false);
    }

    public void HandlePut(object setpoint)
    {
        if (port == null) { Open(); }
        port.Write((bool)setpoint);
    }
}
```

The purpose of this class is to provide a common interface for actuators—namely, a method that consumes new setpoints and is compatible with the delegate type PutHandler, and with a "declarative" initialization mechanism like the one of HttpServer.

# C#: Protecting You from Dangerous Conversions

A variable declared with type `object` accepts anything assigned to it. It is often used in libraries, which should be independent of the exact types that will occur in the various applications that use those libraries. In our case, it is the `Gsiot.Server` library and the `setpoint` parameter of `HandlePut`.

If you know that at some point in your program, a variable of type `object` must contain a value of a particular type, you can cast it safely in the following way:

```
object setpoint = false;        // setpoint now contains a bool value
                                // bool ledSetpoint = (bool)setpoint;
                                // setpoint interpreted as bool value
```

Unlike some other languages, C# will never allow you to proceed with an erroneous type cast on objects. Such type casts will either generate error messages at compile time or exceptions at runtime. In the above example, the check is performed at runtime because the compiler has no way of knowing what you might assign to `ledSetpoint`. By contrast, the following code results in an error at *compile time*:

```
object setpoint = false;        // setpoint now contains a bool value

int boilerSetpoint = setpoint;  // illegal, flagged by compiler
```

The following code results in an exception at *runtime*:

```
object setpoint = false;        // setpoint now contains a bool value

int boilerSetpoint = (int)setpoint;     // throws an exception!
```

As a friend likes to say: every beer bottle is a bottle, but not every bottle is a beer bottle. Similarly, every boiler setpoint is a setpoint (which is an object in turn), but not every setpoint is a boiler setpoint. The C# type system helps to catch many programming mistakes either at compile time or at runtime—and the earlier, the better.

## Inside Gsiot.Server's ManipulatedVariable Class

The library class `ManipulatedVariable` is implemented in namespace `Gsiot.Server`, as shown in Example 12-3.

## Example 12-3. ManipulatedVariable

```
public class ManipulatedVariable
{
    public Deserializer FromHttpRequest { get; set; }
    public PutHandler ToActuator { get; set; }

    public void HandleRequest(RequestHandlerContext context)
    {
        object setpoint;
        if (FromHttpRequest(context, out setpoint))
        {
            // setpoint may be null
            ToActuator(setpoint);
            context.ResponseStatusCode = 200;   // OK
        }
        else
        {
            context.ResponseStatusCode = 400;   // Bad Request
        }
    }
}
```

The purpose of this request handler for manipulated variables is to separate the request processing from the representation used in the request (**FromHttpRequest**) and from the way new setpoints are consumed (**ToActuator**).

# Test Client in C#

To test your **LedController** server with a client that runs on a computer, use the test client given in Example 12-4, which sends a PUT request to the server. You need to adapt the constant **uri** to the address of your device.

The representation sent to the server is contained in constant **message**. See what happens if you send the value as given below, or if you change it to **false** or some unsupported value.

--------------------------------------------------------------------------------

NOTE: This code won't run on a Netduino Plus. You'll have to run it on Windows using .NET, or on Mac OS X or Linux using Mono. Mono is an open source implementation of .NET that runs on several platforms.

--------------------------------------------------------------------------------

# Example 12-4. LedControllerClient test client in C#

```csharp
using System;
using System.IO;
using System.Net;
using System.Text;
using System.Threading;

public class LedControllerClient
{
    public static void Main()
    {
        const string method = "PUT";
        const string uri =
            "http://try.yaler.net/gsiot-FFMQ-TTD5/led/target";
        const string type = "text/plain";
        const string message = "true";   // ignored for GET requests

        HttpWebRequest request = CreateRequest(method, uri, type,
            message);
        try
        {
            using (var response = (HttpWebResponse)request.
                GetResponse())
            {
                LogResponse(response);
            }
        }
        catch (Exception e)
        {
            Console.Write(e.ToString());
            Thread.Sleep(Timeout.Infinite);
        }
    }

    static HttpWebRequest CreateRequest(string method,
        string uri, string type, string body)
    {
        var request = (HttpWebRequest)WebRequest.Create(uri);

        // request line
        request.Method = method;
```

```
if ((body != null) && (method != "GET"))
{
    byte[] buffer = Encoding.UTF8.GetBytes(body);

    // request headers
    request.ContentType = type;
    request.ContentLength = buffer.Length;

    // request body
    using (Stream stream = request.GetRequestStream())
    {
        stream.Write(buffer, 0, buffer.Length);
    }
}
return request;
}

static void LogResponse(HttpWebResponse response)
{
    // response status line
    Console.WriteLine("HTTP/" + response.ProtocolVersion + " " +
        response.StatusDescription);

    // response headers
    string[] headers = response.Headers.AllKeys;
    foreach (string name in headers)
    {
        Console.WriteLine(name + ": " + response.Headers[name]);
    }

    // response body
    var buffer = new byte[response.ContentLength];
    Stream stream = response.GetResponseStream();
    int toRead = buffer.Length;
    while (toRead > 0)
    {
        // already read: buffer.Length - toRead
        int read = stream.Read(buffer, buffer.Length - toRead,
            toRead);
        toRead = toRead - read;
    }
}
```

```
        char[] chars = Encoding.UTF8.GetChars(buffer);
        Console.WriteLine(new string(chars));
        Thread.Sleep(Timeout.Infinite);
    }
}
```

The test client writes the server's response to a console window and then
waits for you to press Ctrl-C to quit it.

# Embed a JavaScript Test Client on the Netduino

Web browsers are convenient HTTP clients because they are available
on practically any platform, and also because they can download new
programs (*scripts*) without extra installation hassles. The trick is that
script code can be embedded in HTML pages, so ordinary HTTP GET
requests are sufficient as download mechanisms for JavaScript
programs. Since JavaScript can issue PUT requests, you can click
buttons on a web page to turn your LEDs on and off!

And since the Netduino Plus is functioning as a web server, you can serve
this JavaScript directly from your .NET Micro Framework code!

To include some JavaScript in an HTML document, add a <script> XML
element with the code shown in Example 12-5. (Example 12-6 shows the
complete example.)

## Example 12-5. LedController test client in JavaScript, embedded in HTML

```
<html>
  <head>
    <script type="text/javascript">
      var r;

      try {
        r = new XMLHttpRequest();
      } catch (e) {
        r = new ActiveXObject('Microsoft.XMLHTTP');
      }
```

```
        function put (content) {
            r.open('PUT', '/gsiot-FFMQ-TTD5/led/target');
            r.setRequestHeader("Content-Type", "text/plain");
            r.send(content);
        }
    </script>
  </head>
  <body>
    <p>
      <input type="button" value="Switch LED on"
        onclick="put('true')"/>
      <input type="button" value="Switch LED off"
        onclick="put('false')"/>
      <input type="button" value="Bah" onclick="put('bah')"/>
    </p>
  </body>
</html>
```

This script creates a new **XMLHttpRequest** object r (short for "request")
or an equivalent *ActiveX* object for Internet Explorer 6 or newer. This
object has a method **open** that takes the HTTP method and the request
URI as parameters, and a method **setRequestHeader** for adding request
headers. It also has a method **send**, which sends the HTTP request back
to your server (your Netduino Plus).

---

NOTE: **XMLHttpRequest** can send any kind of representation, not just XML
as its name suggests.

---

The object r is used in the function **put**, which takes the request message
content as a parameter and sends it back in an HTTP PUT message to the
same server from which the JavaScript came.

The body of the HTML page produces three buttons: Switch LED on,
Switch LED off, and Bah. When you click on them, they call the **put**
function with the arguments **"true"**, **"false"**, or **"bah"**. In the first case,
the request is meant to switch on the Netduino Plus's onboard LED. In
the second case, the request is meant to switch off the Netduino Plus's
onboard LED. In the third case, the request is meant to provoke an error
situation (see the debug console for what happens when you click on it).

The resulting web page looks like Figure 12-2.

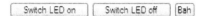

*Figure 12-2. Simple web page for controlling an LED*

The entire program is given in Example 12-6, which encodes the script
from Example 12-5 in one large string. Instead of loading the HTML from a
file, the Netduino Plus will serve it up out of its memory in the body of the
`HandleLedTargetHtml` handler.

## Example 12-6. LedControllerHtml with embedded JavaScript

```
using Gsiot.Server;
using SecretLabs.NETMF.Hardware.NetduinoPlus;

public class LedControllerHtml
{
    public static void Main()
    {
        var ledActuator = new DigitalActuator
        {
            OutputPin = Pins.ONBOARD_LED
        };

        var webServer = new HttpServer
        {
            RelayDomain = "gsiot-FFMQ-TTD5",
            RelaySecretKey =
                "o5fIIZS5tpD2A4Zp87CoKNUsSpIEJZrV5rNjpg89",
            RequestRouting =
            {
                {
                    "PUT /led/target",
                    new ManipulatedVariable
                    {
                        FromHttpRequest =
                            CSharpRepresentation.TryDeserializeBool,
                        ToActuator = ledActuator.HandlePut
                    }.HandleRequest
                },
                {
                    "GET /led/target.html",
```

```
                    HandleLedTargetHtml
            }
        }
    };

    webServer.Run();
}

static void HandleLedTargetHtml(RequestHandlerContext context)
{
    string requestUri = context.BuildRequestUri("/led/target");
    var script =
        @"<html>
            <head>
              <script type=""text/javascript"">
                var r;
                try {
                    r = new XMLHttpRequest();
                } catch (e) {
                    r = new ActiveXObject('Microsoft.XMLHTTP');
                }
                function put (content) {
                    r.open('PUT', '" + requestUri + @"');
                    r.setRequestHeader(""Content-Type"",
                      ""text/plain"");
                    r.send(content);
                }
              </script>
            </head>
            <body>
              <p>
                <input type=""button"" value=""Switch LED on""
                    onclick=""put('true')""/>
                <input type=""button"" value=""Switch LED off""
                    onclick=""put('false')""/>
                <input type=""button"" value=""Bah""
                    onclick=""put('bah')""/>
              </p>
            </body>
          </html>";
    context.SetResponse(script, "text/html");
}
}
```

In this example, note that two resources are supported:

```
{
    "PUT /led/target",
    … request handler …
},
{
    "GET /led/target.html",
    … request handler …
}
```

Another noteworthy aspect of the example is the use of *verbatim strings*. A verbatim string starts with an @ sign and is followed by a " character. It ends at the first " character that isn't doubled. To allow " characters in a verbatim string, two subsequent " characters are interpreted as a single " character. In a verbatim string there may be carriage returns, line feeds, tabulator characters, etc., that don't need an escape sequence like normal strings. This can make verbatim strings more readable in some cases. Here is an example of a verbatim string:

```
string s = @"Hello ""World"" again";
```

It is equivalent to this regular string:

```
string s = "Hello \"World\" again";
```

# What You Should Know About HTTP PUT

To change the state of a device's actuator, you send it HTTP PUT messages. Like GET, PUT is defined as being *idempotent*, meaning that issuing the same PUT request multiple times has the same effect on the server's resources as issuing it only once—assuming no one else changes the same resource. This is particularly relevant in one situation: suppose your client program has sent a PUT request, but it does not get back a response. After a while, the client will time out. What should happen then? If the request had been lost on its way to the server, your client could simply try again and send the PUT request a second time.

But what if the request had been received by the server, was processed correctly, and only the response message got lost somewhere on the way back to your client? Sending the PUT request again would cause the resource to be manipulated a second time. What could be a huge problem is no problem at all if you design your PUT request handlers to be idempotent, in which case simply sending the same PUT request again is harmless. This is the beauty of RESTful web services with HTTP. Distributed systems, where clients and servers operate on different machines and are connected through sometimes-unreliable connections, are notoriously difficult to program correctly. The reason is that unlike single programs on single computers, distributed systems suffer from *partial failures*: one component dies, but the other components continue without knowing what exactly happened. This makes it nearly impossible to recover from failures in such a way that all components are guaranteed to have consistent states again.

The idempotent way in which HTTP GET and PUT (and DELETE) are defined reduces this problem enormously: if a client suspects a problem with a request, it simply repeats it. It doesn't need to find out the current resource state of the server, and it doesn't need to correct it. On the other hand, a server simply responds to a request it receives from a client, and then forgets about this client. It doesn't need to keep track of the client's application state. Whether a client really receives a response message or has died, or whether the message was lost somewhere on the network, need not concern the server. This decoupling of the clients' application states and the servers' resource states is sometimes called *statelessness*.

In practice, this means that almost anything can be a resource—except commands. For example, if you control a loudspeaker's volume with an HTTP server, you can send it a PUT request with a representation of the desired state, e.g., "70%". This is idempotent. You can send it as often as you want; seventy percent remains seventy percent. By contrast, commands are not always idempotent; e.g., "increase volume by one notch" would not be idempotent. Often, a URI name that contains a verb betrays such a mistake, e.g., /loudspeaker/increaseVolume.

# 13/Going Parallel

Imagine that you have written a program that controls some physical process, like rapidly blinking an LED at a fixed frequency. You want to control the parameters of this process through a web service interface, perhaps to adjust the blinking period. This simple scenario raises a far-reaching question. Consider our previous server examples that repeatedly wait for new incoming HTTP requests. Whenever a request arrives, the server wakes up, does something, sends back a response, and then waits again. While it waits, the server *blocks* all other activity until the next request comes in, which may easily take hours. This means that even if you wrote some code to blink the LED, it's not going to blink if the server is sitting around waiting. This is not what you want, of course.

To solve this problem, the .NET Micro Framework provides a very powerful mechanism called *multithreading*. Multithreading is a mechanism for splitting up a program into several parallel activities called *threads*. Each thread provides a single stream of execution, yet they all share the same resources (i.e., they can access the same C# objects). Each of the examples so far used only one thread, which is started implicitly along with the application. Additional threads can be started explicitly, as I will show soon. The point is that while a thread may be waiting due to some blocking call, the others are free to continue (unless they have run into blocking calls themselves).

Multithreading on a single processor is possible thanks to a system service called a *scheduler*, which briefly stops the currently executing thread of an application after each *time slice* (which is 20 milliseconds on the .NET Micro Framework). The scheduler then decides which thread to execute next. It switches among threads in a round-robin fashion so that every thread gets its fair share of processing time. Switching among threads occurs so frequently—50 times per second—that all threads appear to run in parallel.

The scheduler knows which threads are blocked—waiting for some condition to be satisfied—and it only schedules them once the condition is established, e.g., the time for waiting has passed or an HTTP request has arrived. If *all* threads are waiting, the scheduler built into the .NET Micro Framework may put the hardware into a power-saving sleep mode.

Things get interesting when two threads need to work together, because many problems can arise. In the next section, "Multithreading," I will discuss thread creation and communication among threads in more detail, including the major causes of problems and a possible way to address them. Afterwards, in the section "ParallelBlinker," I will provide a complete example.

# Multithreading

Multithreading makes it possible for two or more activities to execute in parallel on a single processor. In .NET, an object of type Thread in the namespace System.Threading represents and controls one thread. Its constructor takes a parameterless method as a parameter (a delegate—see Chapter 11 for more details). This method will be executed later, once the thread's Start method is called.

In Example 13-1, thread1 will execute EvenActivity, and thread2 will execute OddActivity. The main thread of the application is blocked forever by calling Thread.Sleep(Timeout.Infinite) after the two new threads are started.

## Example 13-1. TwoThreads

```
using System.Threading;
using Microsoft.SPOT;

public class TwoThreads
{
    public static void Main()
    {
        var thread1 = new Thread(EvenActivity);
        var thread2 = new Thread(OddActivity);

        thread1.Start();
        thread2.Start();

        Thread.Sleep(Timeout.Infinite);
    }

    static void EvenActivity()
    {
        var x = 0;      // even number
        while (true)
```

```
        {
            Debug.Print(x.ToString());
            x = x + 2;
            Thread.Sleep(200);
        }
    }

    static void OddActivity()
    {
        var x = 1;        // odd number
        while (true)
        {
            Debug.Print("      " + x);
            x = x + 2;
            Thread.Sleep(300);
        }
    }
}
```

EvenActivity contains an endless loop that prints out a sequence of
even numbers; OddActivity prints a sequence of odd numbers. The first
outputs of a run may look like this:

```
0
        1
2
4
        3
6
        5
8
10
        7
12
        9
14
16
        11
18
        13
20
22
        15
```

Even if one of the threads is sleeping (i.e., blocked), the other can execute. This is the reason why I will use multiple threads later in `ParallelBlinker` (Example 13-5).

Multithreading is so powerful that it gives you a lot of rope to hang yourself. In the following two sections, I sketch the two most important pitfalls of multithreading: race conditions and deadlocks. Just as Odysseus had to find his way between Scylla and Charybdis, you'll have to navigate between these monsters. Without the right guidelines, you'll run into one or both; with the tricks I will show you later in this chapter, you can sail peacefully between them. See Figure 13-1 for inspiration.

*Figure 13-1. Beware of Scylla and Charybdis*

## Beware of Scylla: Race Conditions

If the result of a program depends on the timing of its parts, it can suffer from *race conditions*. Consider the following statements:

```
int x = 1;
if (x != 1) { throw new Exception(); }
```

This code assigns the value 1 to variable x, and then checks whether x has indeed become 1; otherwise, it throws an exception. Of course, there should never be an exception because one of the most basic assumptions in programming is that after an assignment x = value, the condition x == value is true.

This solid ground turns into quicksand as soon as you use more than one thread. Consider Example 13-2. It has a static variable x and two threads that repeatedly modify x. One of them sets x to 0; the other sets it to 1. Immediately after setting x, a thread checks whether x indeed has the assigned value.

## Example 13-2. TwoThreadsAtTheRaces

```
using System;
using System.Threading;

public class TwoThreadsAtTheRaces
{
    static int x;

    public static void Main()
    {
        var thread1 = new Thread(Activity1);
        var thread2 = new Thread(Activity2);

        thread1.Start();
        thread2.Start();

        Thread.Sleep(Timeout.Infinite);
    }

    static void Activity1()
    {
        while (true)
        {
            x = 0;
            if (x != 0) { throw new Exception(); }
        }
    }

    static void Activity2()
    {
        while (true)
        {
            x = 1;
```

```
            if (x != 1) { throw new Exception(); }
        }
    }
}
```

When you run this program, it will soon stop with an exception, either in `Activity1` or `Activity2`. Let's assume it was `Activity1`. The explanation is simple: the scheduler must have switched from `Activity1` to `Activity2` right after the statement `x = 0`. `Activity2` then executed its loop a zillion times, always setting `x` to 1 and verifying that it has indeed become 1, until 20 milliseconds have passed. Then `Activity1` resumes, by checking whether `x` is `0`, which it isn't, so an exception is thrown. After the program is started, it is only a matter of time until this exact scenario plays out.

Thus, the art lies in writing multithreaded programs that do not depend on the vagaries of timing, and will therefore never produce random-looking effects due to race conditions.

Shared variables like `x` in Example 13-2 are the source of the problem, but you cannot always avoid using shared variables. Fortunately, there are mechanisms to protect shared variables from uncoordinated accesses by different threads.

In C#, the `lock` statement can be used to temporarily reserve some variables for one thread, as shown in Example 13-3. The lock's statement sequence is called a *critical section*. If used correctly, locks make sure that there is never more than one thread executing until the completion of a critical section. For example, if thread X is in this critical section:

```
lock (monitor) { critical section }
```

and thread Y tries to enter the same critical section by calling `lock (monitor)`, then thread Y is blocked until X has left the critical section. From then on, Y is free to continue, locking the critical section for itself.

The `lock` statement requires an object reference as an argument. I create a `monitor` object solely for this purpose. It is not marked as `public`; this is to ensure that no other class is able to provoke a deadlock (see the following section).

# Example 13-3. TwoThreadsInTheLocks

```
using System;
using System.Threading;

public class TwoThreadsInTheLocks
{
    static int x = 0;

    static object monitor = new object();

    public static void Main()
    {
        var thread1 = new Thread(Activity1);
        var thread2 = new Thread(Activity2);

        thread1.Start();
        thread2.Start();

        Thread.Sleep(Timeout.Infinite);
    }

    static void Activity1()
    {
        while (true)
        {
            lock (monitor)
            {
                x = 0;
                if (x != 0) { throw new Exception(); }
            }
        }
    }

    static void Activity2()
    {
        while (true)
        {
            lock (monitor)
```

```
            {
                x = 1;
                if (x != 1) { throw new Exception(); }
            }
        }
    }
}
```

If you run this program, it will not end up in an exception. Reconsider our scenario from earlier: `Activity1` has just executed x = 0 right before the current time slice has elapsed. The scheduler switches to `Activity2`. `Activity2` calls `lock(monitor)`. Since `Activity1` has already locked the critical section guarded by `monitor`, the scheduler backs off and gives control to another thread. Since `Activity1` is the only other thread ready to be executed, `Activity1` regains control and continues. The test x != 0 yields false, since `Activity2` never had the chance to change x to 1. No exception is thrown. And so on.

Thus the rules for avoiding race conditions are:

1. Protect all shared variables by using locks.

2. Minimize the danger of overlooking such variables by minimizing the number of variables visible to multiple threads.

3. Keep critical sections as short as possible.

4. Perform as few method calls as possible in critical sections. In particular, don't call any method that may block. Which leads us to Charybdis...

## Beware of Charybdis: Deadlocks

Locking keeps you away from the Scylla called race conditions. Beware that it doesn't drive you into the arms of the Charybdis: *deadlock*.

Consider two threads X and Y that both need access to the same two variables, `variableA` and `variableB`. One set is protected by `monitorA`, the other by `monitorB`. Thread X contains the following code:

```
lock (monitorA)
{
    lock (monitorB)
```

```
    {
        // now use variableA and variableB
    }
}
```

Thread Y, on the other hand, contains this code:

```
lock (monitorB)
{
    lock (monitorA)
    {
        // now use variableA and variableB
    }
}
```

If it now happens—and eventually it probably will—that thread X has locked monitorA but the scheduler passes control to thread Y right afterwards, Y locks monitorB and proceeds to lock monitorA. Because X already locked monitorA, Y is blocked, and the scheduler tries to find another thread ready to be executed. X is ready, and it proceeds by trying to lock monitorB. Because Y already locked monitorB, X is blocked, and the scheduler needs to find yet another thread ready to be executed—only there isn't one left. X and Y have ended up in a deadlock, where each one can proceed only if the other proceeds.

If both threads had tried to lock monitorA first and monitorB second (or the other way around), the problem wouldn't occur. However, in large applications, it becomes very difficult to guarantee the same sequence of locking in all places, particularly if the thread crisscrosses different methods—of your own code and library code—or calls delegates where you don't know beforehand what code they will be bound to, etc. Any blocking call may internally use some lock that is invisible to you.

The solution: if possible, avoid using multiple locks; instead, use one "big" global lock. If there exists only one lock, there cannot be deadlocks.

## Stay in Calmer Waters: Actors

Too little locking provokes race conditions; too much locking provokes deadlocks. One discipline for staying in the calm(er) waters between Scylla and Charybdis is to limit interaction among threads to a mechanism that hides all the locking. Such a thread may access only its own variables. Where it needs to cooperate with other threads, it puts messages into buffers or gets messages from buffers. These buffers are implemented in library classes that perform all necessary locking. Here are the golden rules of this programming style:

» "My state is my castle"

The objects of an application are assigned to *actors* so that every object belongs to exactly *one* actor. An actor is itself an object that has its own thread. This thread must access only objects of its own actor, thereby avoiding any interference among threads. Ideally, the objects of an actor are encapsulated within the actor object, making them invisible to other actors and their threads. With this scheme, no race conditions or deadlocks can occur. A "castle" is a good analogy because the subjects of a castle live within the castle walls—or at least on grounds that clearly belong to the castle.

» "I stay in my castle"

An actor and its objects must not have references to anything that does not belong to this actor *exclusively*. If you cannot avoid calling system libraries, make sure that they cannot cause you to stray outside of your castle inadvertently.

» "I communicate through letters"

As an exception to the "I stay in my castle" rule, buffers implemented by a trusted system library may be used by several actors. An actor may contain references to such buffers, and it may put messages to or get messages from them. Unlike actors, buffers don't have their own threads, but they internally perform locking such that parallel access by several actors is safe. Buffers are the glue between actors, channeling the flow of data between them.

» "I fire and forget"

An actor must not keep any references to data that it has put into a buffer. If it needs to keep the data, it puts an independent *copy* of all the data in the buffer. Otherwise, there would suddenly be two actors that—directly or indirectly—refer to the same object, thereby violating the "I stay in my castle" rule (and thus are bound to produce race conditions). Think of putting a message into a buffer as a complete handover of the message and all its contents.

The program structure of such an actor program looks as shown in Example 13-4.

## Example 13-4. Common actor program outline

```
// using directives

public class MyApplication
{
    public static void Main()
    {
        // buffers for the communication between actors
        //      create and set up threadsafe buffers

        // actor 1, e.g., an actor that samples sensor S1
        //      create and set up actor and its helper objects

        // actor 2, e.g., an actor that samples sensors S2 and S3
        //      create and set up actor and its helper objects

        ...

        // actor n, e.g., an actor that controls actuator A3
        //      create and set up actor and its helper objects

        // web interface
        // create and set up actor that implements a web interface

        // start threads for actors 1 to n
        // use main thread for web actor
    }
}
```

The main challenge here is to make sure that it always remains clear which objects belong to which actor. This is necessary to guarantee that an actor always touches only its own objects, or the threadsafe buffers.

# ParallelBlinker

ParallelBlinker is a complete example with one actor called blinker that periodically blinks the onboard LED, and another called webServer that handles HTTP requests. Once running, both actors, shown in Figure 13-2, communicate only through the buffer variable. It is the boundary between the two actors.

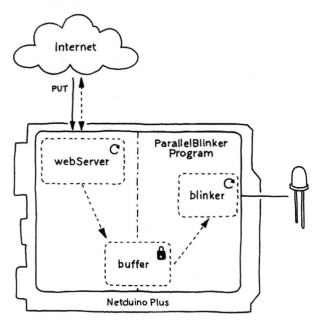

*Figure 13-2. Architecture of ParallelBlinker*

The complete program is given in Example 13-5.

## Example 13-5. ParallelBlinker

```
using System.Threading;
using Gsiot.Server;
using Microsoft.SPOT.Hardware;
using SecretLabs.NETMF.Hardware.NetduinoPlus;

public class ParallelBlinker
{
    public static void Main()
```

```
{
    var buffer = new Buffer { };

    var blinker = new Blinker { SourceBuffer = buffer };

    var webServer = new HttpServer
    {
        RelayDomain = "gsiot-FFMQ-TTD5",
        RelaySecretKey =
            "o5fIIZS5tpD2A4Zp87CoKNUsSpIEJZrV5rNjpg89",
        RequestRouting =
        {
            {
                "PUT /blinkingPeriod/target",
                new ManipulatedVariable
                {
                    FromHttpRequest =
                        CSharpRepresentation.TryDeserializeInt,
                    ToActuator = buffer.HandlePut
                }.HandleRequest
            },
            {
                "GET /blinkingPeriod/target.html",
                HandleBlinkTargetHtml
            }
        }
    };

    var blinkerThread = new Thread(blinker.Run);
    blinkerThread.Start();
    webServer.Run();
}

static void HandleBlinkTargetHtml(RequestHandlerContext context)
{
    string requestUri =
        context.BuildRequestUri("/blinkingPeriod/target");
    var script =
        @"<html>
            <head>
              <script type=""text/javascript"">
                var r;
                try {
```

```
            r = new XMLHttpRequest();
        } catch (e) {
            r = new ActiveXObject('Microsoft.XMLHTTP');
        }
        function put (content) {
            r.open('PUT', '" + requestUri + @"');
            r.setRequestHeader(""Content-Type"",
              ""text/plain"");
            r.send(document.getElementById(""period"").
              value);
        }
    </script>
</head>
<body>
    <p>
        <input type=""text"" value=""500"" id=""period"">
        <input
          type=""button"" value=""Set""
            onclick=""put()""/>
    </p>
</body>
</html>";
    context.SetResponse(script, "text/html");
    }
}


public class Blinker
{
    public Buffer SourceBuffer { get; set; }

    public void Run()
    {
        var ledPort = new OutputPort(Pins.ONBOARD_LED, false);
        var period = 500;
        var on = true;
        while (true)
        {
            Thread.Sleep(period / 2);

            object setpoint = SourceBuffer.HandleGet();
            if (setpoint != null)
```

```
    {
        period = (int)setpoint;
        period = period > 10000 ? 10000 : period;
        period = period < 20 ? 20 : period;
    }


    on = !on;
    ledPort.Write(on);
        }
    }
}
```

We only need one buffer, which is used to communicate a new setpoint (see Chapter 12) for the blinking period to the blinker actor. The Buffer type (from namespace Gsiot.Server) is a simple buffer where one actor calls HandlePut to put a new setpoint in it, and another actor calls HandleGet to retrieve it from there. When a new setpoint is put in the buffer, it overwrites any old value that was put there earlier.

Since a new blinking period is a setpoint for the blinker object, we use a ManipulatedVariable for representing the blinking period, with the URI /blinkingPeriod/target. We assume that this is an integer value represented as plain text, so we can use CSharpRepresentation. TryDeserializeInt for the conversion from an HTTP message body to a C# object. Once such a conversion has happened, the resulting object is put in the buffer by calling buffer.HandlePut.

The Blinker class has one property, SourceBuffer, which is its reference to the buffer. It treats it as a source, since this is where the new setpoints come from. Whenever the blinker thread awakens, it tries to get a new setpoint from this buffer. If there is one, it converts it to an integer value and makes sure that the value is not larger than 10,000 and not smaller than 20 (these are completely arbitrary values; you would probably use different ones). Then the state of the LED is toggled.

As a user interface for the program, ParallelBlinker supports a resource /blinkingPeriod/target.html, which returns a web page where you can type in a target value for the blinking period.

# What You Should Know About Multithreading

Using multithreading is simple. Using it *correctly* isn't. It's like a sword that consists of only a sharp, double-edged blade and no handle: it cuts anything, and usually starts by cutting the one who carries it. I have briefly explained race conditions and deadlocks, but there are even more subtle issues with strange names such as livelock, fairness, starvation, and—worst of all—memory models.

Your program may reliably work on the current version of a .NET implementation even if it contains multithreading errors. But those errors might break things on another .NET implementation, on the next release of the same implementation, or even on the same .NET implementation executed on another processor architecture. So you can sometimes get away with code that contains minor errors at first, but you'll run into trouble eventually.

There seem to exist hardly any multithreaded programs that are fully correct. Even experts often make mistakes. Debugging is almost impossible, since problems often cannot be reproduced. This highly annoying nondeterminism of parallel programs has its roots in the modification of shared state by multiple threads. To reduce the likelihood for trouble, you must minimize the number of different threads and the number of shared variables.

The simple actor programming style I have used in this chapter should keep you away from trouble. It isolates shared state by keeping it in buffers, which are provided by my (hopefully correct) `Gsiot.Server.Buffer` class. Using a thread for every actor is not the most efficient implementation of an actor model, but it can be reasonable for a small number of actors.

If you want to use threads in more aggressive ways, I recommend that you first study the .NET-related parts of Joe Duffy's book, *Concurrent Programming on Windows* (Addison-Wesley).

# 14/Where Can I Go from Here?

The title of this book is *Getting Started with the Internet of Things*, and I hope that it *did* help you take the first steps. You may now be wondering where to go next. In this chapter, I compiled some things that might be of interest to you.

## Recipes for Modifying a Server

Now that you have seen several example servers for monitoring sensors and for controlling actuators, it's possible to make various changes to such a server (illustrated in Figure 14-1). I mainly discuss sensors and measured variables, but actuators and manipulated variables can be handled in the same way (if not stated otherwise).

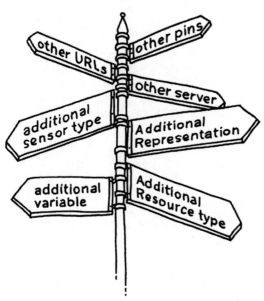

*Figure 14-1. Various ways to change a server*

## Changing the Pin Assignment of a Sensor

If you have moved a physical sensor from one pin to another, go to the corresponding sensor object and change the pin. For example, if you want to move the potentiometer of Example 11-1, `VoltageMonitor`, one pin position to the right, change the `InputPin` property of `voltageSensor` from `Pins.GPIO_PIN_A1` to `Pins.GPIO_PIN_A2`. (And for this example, don't forget to move `highPort` and `lowPort` as well, or use other ways to provide power and ground to the potentiometer.) The pins of the Netduino Plus that are accessible through connectors are listed in Table 2-1 in Chapter 2.

## Changing the URI of a Measured Variable

If you want to change the particular URI of a measured variable, go to the `webServer` object in the `Main` method and change the request pattern for the variable, e.g., from `"GET /voltage/actual"` to `"GET /potentiometer/actual"`.

## Adding a New Measured Variable

If you want to add a new measured variable, go to the `Main` method, add a new sensor variable, and then add a corresponding `MeasuredVariable` object to the server object.

For example, add a variable:

```
var garageDoorSensor = new DigitalSensor
{
    InputPin = Pins.GPIO_PIN_D0
};
```

and then the measured variable:

```
var webServer = new HttpServer
{
    RelayDomain = "gsiot-FFMQ-TTD5",
    RelaySecretKey = "o5fIIZS5tpD2A4Zp87CoKNUsSpIEJZrV5rNjpg89",
    RequestRouting =
    {
        {
            "GET /voltage/actual",
            new MeasuredVariable
```

```
        {
            FromSensor = voltageSensor.HandleGet
        }.HandleRequest
    },
    {

        "/garageDoor/actual",
        new MeasuredVariable
        {
            FromSensor = garageDoorSensor.HandleGet
        }.HandleRequest
    }
  }
};
```

## Adding a New Type of Sensor

If you want to add a measured variable for an entirely new type of sensor that is not already provided by Gsiot.Server, you need to develop your own sensor class. For example, an analog sensor for voltage values that uses the same trick for providing power and ground, as shown in Chapter 3, could look like this:

```
public class MySpecialPotentiometerSensor
{
    public Cpu.Pin InputPin { get; set; }
    public Cpu.Pin LowOutputPin { get; set; }
    public Cpu.Pin HighOutputPin { get; set; }

    AnalogInput voltagePort;
    OutputPort lowPort;
    OutputPort highPort;

    const double maxVoltage = 3.3;
    const int maxAdcValue = 1023;

    public void Open()
    {
        voltagePort = new AnalogInput(InputPin);
        lowPort = new OutputPort(LowOutputPin, false);
        highPort = new OutputPort(HighOutputPin, true);
    }
```

```
        public object HandleGet()
        {
            if (voltagePort == null) { Open(); }
            int rawValue = voltagePort.Read();
            double value = (rawValue * maxVoltage) / maxAdcValue;
            return value;
        }
    }
```

You could pack your sensor and actuator classes in a separate driver library or simply add them after the application program:

```
// using directives

public class MyApplication
{
    public static void Main()
    {
        // create and initialize buffer, sensor, actuator objects

        var webServer = new HttpServer
        {
            …
        };

        // create and start threads
        webServer.Run();
    }
}

public class MySpecialPotentiometerSensor
{
    …
}

// other sensor or actuator classes
```

When designing a sensor class, the only requirement is that it provides some public method that has no parameters and returns a sample of type object. As a convention, it is called HandleGet. As a further convention, configuration parameters are provided as properties and, if necessary, a parameterless method Open is provided for initialization.

NOTE: Actuators provide a method `HandlePut`.

You still face a tough design challenge: which properties should your driver objects expose for configuration purposes? The temptation is to provide properties for all conceivable circumstances, thereby committing design overkill.

My recommendation is to start with only those properties that you definitely need. If you keep the class small, it will be easy to extend if and when necessary. Once it has gotten too large, it tends to become difficult to strip down to something smaller again. So, keep your driver classes as simple and small as possible. The limited code space of a Netduino Plus is of course another incentive to keep things small.

## Adding a New Kind of Resource

If you want to add a resource that is neither a measured variable nor a manipulated variable, you have to provide a request handler for it. This can be a class with arbitrary configuration properties and a `HandleRequest` method, more or less similar to `MeasuredVariable` and `ManipulatedVariable`. An instance of such a class can handle more than one resource—e.g., a hypothetical **Feed** class might support a resource for the actual value, several resources for the feed history, a resource that describes the feed, etc. Because these resources all have different URIs, a request handler can also be regarded as an interpreter for a special-purpose URI language.

If you do not need any configuration state for a request handler, you don't have to provide a class. A simple method is sufficient, as shown in the following example that assumes the request pattern "* /*", which matches any request:

```
static void HandleGetAbout(RequestHandlerContext context)
{
    if (context.RequestUri == "/about")
    {
        if (context.RequestMethod == "GET")
        {
            var s = "This is a device programmed in C#";
            context.SetResponse(s, "text/plain");
        }
        else
```

```
        {
            context.ResponseStatusCode = 405;   // MethodNotAllowed
        }
    }
    else if (context.RequestUri == "/about.html")
    {
        if (context.RequestMethod == "GET")
        {
            var s =
                @"<html>
                    This is a device programmed in
                    <strong>C#</strong>
                    </html>";
            context.SetResponse(s, "text/html");
        }
        else
        {
            context.ResponseStatusCode = 405;   // MethodNotAllowed
        }
    }
}
```

## Supporting a New Representation for a Measured Variable

So far, I have only used the default CSharpRepresentation class for converting between HTTP message bodies and C# objects. Obviously, there is a need to support other representations. My simple server library supports text representations such as plain text (text/plain), comma-separated value lists (text/csv), HTML (text/html), XML (application/xml), JSON (application/json), and similar formats.

For example, you might use the following (optional) initializer to provide a more browser-friendly representation, assuming you have written a suitable class HtmlRepresentation:

```
{
    "GET /voltage/actual",
    new MeasuredVariable
    {
        FromSensor = voltageSensor.HandleGet,
        ToHttpRequest = HtmlRepresentation.Serialize
```

```
}.HandleRequest
}
```

If you studied the section "Inside Gsiot.Server's MeasuredVariable Class" in Chapter 11, you may have noticed that I presented a somewhat simplified version, without a `ToHttpRequest` property. Likewise, some other classes in `Gsiot.Server` also have a few additional features not used in the examples, though they're explained in Appendix C.

## Replacing the Server Implementation

The server in my `Gsiot.Server` library is very simple and still quite flexible. If its flexibility is not sufficient, another server can replace it, as long as the new one also supports `RequestHandler` delegates in some way.

# Server Versus Client? When to Push, When to Pull?

You may have asked yourself, "When should I program a device as a server, and when as a client?" Should you push samples to a server, as with the Pachube clients in Part II, or should you have clients pull samples from your device as a server, as in Part III? There is no hard and fast rule for this decision. There are good arguments for both approaches, and your particular situation usually determines which way the scales tip.

Making the device a *client* is an obvious choice if someone must be notified without any delay whenever the device detects some alarm condition. Making the device a *server* is an obvious choice if a user must be able to control an actuator, or the device's configuration, without any delay. If both of these things are required simultaneously, the device should be both client and server at the same time.

Making a device both client and server is perfectly possible. However, this can be a rather heavy burden for a small device. Fortunately, the requirements are usually less stringent. After all, the Internet does not guarantee that it delivers every message, let alone the maximum time that a delivery takes. So a hard real-time maximum duration for the delivery of measurements, alarms, commands, or new configurations cannot be expected anyway. This means that you often have the choice to make a device either client or server. In many cases, a closer look at the specific circumstances will lead to a clear preference for one or the other solution. For example, the costs for data communication over a mobile phone connection could make the push approach so expensive that it becomes unattractive. On the other hand, a battery-powered device may drain the battery too quickly if it runs a server that is always "on."

If there is still no clear winner, you can comfortably decide based on which approach is simpler to implement and takes fewer resources on the device. Maybe surprisingly, the "device as HTTP client" approach is often more cumbersome and bulky than the "device as HTTP server" approach. This has to do with the fact that an HTTP server is king over its resources. To exaggerate somewhat: a client can only plea by sending a request; the server decides whether it likes the request and how it will respond. The client has to be prepared for a whole set of possible server responses. For example, the server's response to a GET request may be "go look somewhere else for this resource" by setting the response status code to `301 Moved Permanently` or a related status code (HTTP redirection). Then, the client has to repeat the request with a different URI. It can be quite tricky to implement a client that correctly responds to all possible server responses.

# Taking a REST

When you start designing your own Internet of Things application, in particular your own on-device web service, there will come a time when you wonder, "But is this a good design?" As the Web has shown, its underlying REST principles are a solid basis for good Internet applications. The core idea of REST is simple:

> Access resources by sending HTTP messages that contain appropriate representations.

When you design a RESTful web service interface, the meat of your design work should not be in designing the URIs of the resources, but in designing the representations of the resources (see Chapter 4). Ideally, you can use an already existing, standardized representation such as HTML or the ATOM format that is used for many RSS feeds. Sometimes you will have to design your own representation. Then, it helps to base your representation on existing conventions, e.g., by using a comma-separated value format, or JSON for more complicated data. Someone who knows HTTP, plus the resource URIs of your service, should only have to learn about the representations to be used in HTTP requests and responses. While this sounds simple, for most people it takes some getting used to. It certainly did for me, but it was worthwhile.

# Communities

Reading books is one way to learn about things—participating in communities is another. For the Netduino Plus, there is a very active online community at *http://forums.netduino.com/*. It is friendly toward newbies and a great place to learn by reading about other people's projects. You can also allow others to learn from your experiences by writing about your own projects.

A NETMF online community that is not dedicated to a particular hardware platform is Microsoft's site, *http://www.netmf.com*. The Microsoft engineers who created NETMF are involved in this site, along with many other users.

Another NETMF community, for the users of hardware from GHI Electronics (see the next section), is at *http://www.tinyclr.com/*.

# Other Hardware

For the examples in this book, I have used little more than the onboard hardware of a Netduino Plus, plus a tacked-on potentiometer, so that we could concentrate on the core topic: namely, the interaction of devices over the Internet. But after taking the first steps, there are additional things you may want to do—for example, to attach other sensors and actuators to your Netduino Plus, to use other communication channels such as serial connections, or to use more powerful processors than what the Netduino Plus provides. In this section, I give an overview of the various possibilities that you have.

## Sensors, Actuators, and Other Hardware Extensions

Most interfaces for simple sensors boil down to measuring electrical voltages or electrical currents. Interfaces for more complex sensors typically provide some kind of serial connections, using a variety of protocols. For example, you can obtain location data from most GPS modules in the text-based *NMEA* protocol (*http://www.gpsinformation.org/dale/nmea.htm*). In any case, it may be possible to attach a sensor (or actuator) to your Netduino Plus by directly inserting wires into the connectors on the board, by plugging a shield into these connectors, or by leading wires from these connectors to a breakout board into which you can stick all kinds of electrical circuits (no soldering needed!). For example, I stuck the potentiometer of Chapter 3 directly into the Netduino Plus connectors. If it hadn't fit those connectors, I would have used a breadboard or the MakerShield (*http://www.makershed.com/ProductDetails.asp?ProductCode=MSMS01*).

The Netduino Plus connectors are compatible, mechanically and electrically, with those of the popular Arduino. This means that many Arduino-compatible shields are hardware-compatible with the Netduino Plus. For software compatibility, some kind of driver is often needed. One of the great advantages of NETMF is that it provides simple object-oriented hardware abstractions, like the `InputPort` and `OutputPort` classes for GPIOs, which can be used for writing your own driver in C#. Various drivers for Arduino shields have been written by the Netduino community. You can view the list of compatible shields at *http://forums.netduino.com/index.php?/forum/4-netduino/*.

## Different Processor Boards

The Netduino board family is a great platform for applications where low cost per device is important and where the available memory is sufficient. However, Netduinos are by no means the only game in town. Even assuming that you want to stay with the .NET Micro Framework, there are various other boards available.

An example of a medium-performance board is the EMX Development System (*http://www.ghielectronics.com/catalog/product/129*) from GHI Electronics. This board features 16 MB of RAM, a 72 MHz ARM 7 microcontroller, Ethernet, 320 x 240 pixel LCD screen, a battery-backed real-time clock, plus various extension ports. GHI Electronics also sells several lower-cost boards, called FEZ products (*http://www.ghielectronics.com/catalog/category/37/*).

An example of a high-performance board is the Topaz i.MX25 (*http://devicesolutions.net/Products/TopaziMX25DevelopmentKit.aspx*) from Device Solutions. This board features 64 MB of RAM, a 400 MHz ARM 9 processor, Ethernet, and much more.

Other NETMF-compatible products can be found in the hardware showcase at *http://www.netmf.com*. This broad spectrum of capabilities at different price points makes NETMF very attractive from the perspective of hardware choices.

## Porting the .NET Micro Framework

One question that inevitably comes up during discussions of NETMF hardware is, "Can I port NETMF to hardware X myself?" If you have the necessary expertise, you could indeed do this, because everything needed is open source. But beware: this is nontrivial, and requires both hardware and firmware experience.

Nevertheless, to give you at least an idea of what is involved, I've provided a short summary. To do a complete port for a new core, three steps are required:

» New core

Let's assume that you want to support a processor core for which there is no NETMF port available. For example, at the time of this writing, there is no NETMF port available for the increasingly popular ARM Cortex-M3 core. First, you need to start with Microsoft's sources, choose a suitable C/C++ compiler for this core, and select a development board with debugging support. The main challenges here are the core initializations: interrupts, reset and error handling, caches, memory management units, etc.

» Same core, new chip

You cannot buy a core by itself—you always buy a complete chip. For example, you can buy the STMicroelectronics STM32F217VG microcontroller, which contains a Cortex-M3 core. Then, you take the existing core software described above and develop drivers for the peripherals of the microcontroller: digital inputs and outputs (GPIO); analog inputs and outputs; various serial communication interfaces and buses, from UARTs to USB and maybe even Ethernet; internal Flash; external RAM; power management; real-time clock; timers; LCD with or without touch screen support; camera interfaces; and so on. These drivers form the hardware-abstraction layer of NETMF.

» Same chip, new board

If you buy a board with a chip for which you already have the necessary drivers and core software, all you need to do is to configure it for this particular board. Basically, this means specifying how much memory is available at which addresses, and which peripherals are attached to which pins. Programming is only required if you have to write high-level drivers for interfacing with other components on the board, e.g., with a serial Flash chip, or with a WiFi or GPS module.

If you already have experience with embedded programming and know NETMF well, a few weeks or even days might be sufficient for the "same chip, new board" step. However, if you have to go through all three steps, it will take you about half a year of full-time work (assuming you are an experienced embedded developer).

You might even develop your own board, ideally using the "same chip, new board" approach. For example, you may start with the open source Netduino Plus schematics, board layout, and NETMF port (*http://www.netduino.com/downloads/*).

# The Sky Is the Limit

Today, the Internet of Things is in an embryonic state. No one knows how it will evolve, what applications will become successful, and which ideas will collapse. This is the time for makers, for trying out projects that nobody else has thought of yet. As Figure 14-2 illustrates, you can boldly go where no developer has gone before!

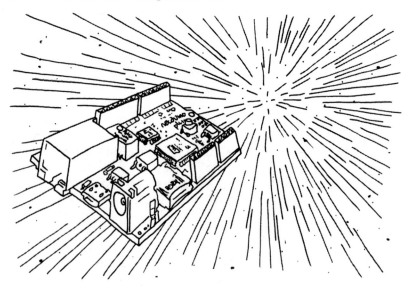

*Figure 14-2. The sky is the limit!*

# A/Test Server

For testing applications that send or receive HTTP messages, i.e., HTTP *clients*, you can use suitable tools for logging HTTP traffic, such as *Wireshark* (*http://www.wireshark.org/*) or *Fiddler* (*http://www.fiddler2.com/*). However, before issuing HTTP requests to a real web service out in the wild, you may want to know beforehand exactly *what* you would send. A simple test server is often all that you need. You run your client program (e.g., `SimplePutRequest`, Example 7-1), on your Netduino Plus, and you run a .NET test server that logs an incoming request on your development PC.

In your client program for the Netduino Plus, change the request URI to something like this:

```
http://192.168.5.100:8080/testHello
```

but replace *192.168.5.100* with the Internet address of your PC. You can find this address by following these steps on Windows:

1.  Start the command prompt application at Start→All Programs→Accessories→Command Prompt.

2.  Type in the string `ipconfig`, and then press Enter.

In the resulting output, your PC's Internet address is called `IP Address`.

To view the IP address on the Mac, open System Preferences, click Network, and select an active (green) network adapter. On Linux, you can open a Terminal and use the `ipconfig` command to view IP addresses for your network adapters.

A simple test server (Example A-1) receives HTTP requests and writes them to a console window. The response that it sends back to the client has status code 200 (OK).

---

NOTE: This code won't run on a Netduino Plus. You'll have to run it on Windows using .NET, or on Mac OS X or Linux using Mono. Mono is an open source implementation of .NET that runs on several platforms.

---

# Example A-1. TestServer

```
using System;
using System.IO;
using System.Net;

class TestServer
{
    static void Main()
    {
        var httpPort = new HttpListener();
        // handle every request that has a request URI starting
        // with "http://" and ending with ":8080/", i.e., anything
        // addressed to port 8080
        httpPort.Prefixes.Add("http://+:8080/");
        httpPort.Start();

        while (true)
        {
            try
            {
                HttpListenerContext context = httpPort.GetContext();
                LogRequest(context.Request);
                HandleRequest(context);
                context.Response.Close();
            }
            catch (Exception e)
            {
                Console.WriteLine(e.ToString());
            }
        }
    }

    static void HandleRequest(HttpListenerContext context)
    {
        context.Response.StatusCode = (int)HttpStatusCode.OK;
        // set up an appropriate content if necessary
    }
```

```
static void LogRequest(HttpListenerRequest request)
{

    // request line
    Console.WriteLine(request.HttpMethod + " " +
                      request.RawUrl + " " +
                      "HTTP/" + request.ProtocolVersion);

    // request headers
    foreach (String name in request.Headers)
    {
        Console.WriteLine(name + ": " + request.Headers[name]);
    }

    // request body
    Console.WriteLine();
    var buffer = new byte[request.ContentLength64];
    Stream stream = request.InputStream;
    int toRead = buffer.Length;
    while (toRead > 0)
    {
        // already read: buffer.Length - toRead
        int read = stream.Read(buffer, buffer.Length - toRead,
            toRead);
        toRead = toRead - read;
    }
    Console.WriteLine(request.ContentEncoding.GetString(buffer));
    }
}
```

This **TestServer** utility program is actually a true web server, using the
server-side classes of the **System.Net** namespace, in particular
**HttpListener**, **HttpListenerRequest**, and **HttpListenerResponse**.

---

NOTE: When you build **TestServer**, make sure that it is compiled as a
Console application for the full .NET Framework, not for NETMF!

---

Open port 8080 in your PC's firewall. To do this on Windows:

1. Select Start→Control Panel.

2. In the Control Panel, click on Windows Firewall (on Windows 7, you'll find this under "System and Security").

3. In the Windows Firewall dialog box, click on the Exceptions tab (on Windows 7, click Advanced Settings).

4. In the Exceptions tab, click on the button Add Port (on Windows 7, first left-click and then right-click Inbound Rules, choose New Rule, then select Port and click Next).

5. In the "Add a Port" dialog box, enter a name in the Name field, and enter 8080 in the Port number field. Make sure that TCP is selected. Then click the OK button. (On Windows 7, the Name field doesn't appear until the last step; choose TCP and type the port number, click Next, select "Allow the Connection", and click Next again.)

6. By clicking on the Change Scope button, you can limit incoming requests to your home network by selecting "My network (subnet) only". (On Windows 7, you can choose to activate it on any combination of Domain, Private, and Public networks.)

7. Start TestServer before the client sends an HTTP message.

If you don't open port 8080 as described above, the client program will run into an exception with the 10053 socket error code. This is because the firewall prevents it from opening a connection to TestServer.

If everything works, you should see the request sent by your Netduino Plus on your PC, in a console or Terminal window.

# B/.NET Classes Used in the Examples

The following tables list the classes used in the NETMF examples, with their respective namespaces and assemblies.

Table B-1 gives the classes Microsoft created for .NET or the .NET Micro Framework.

*Table B-1. .NET Micro Framework classes*

| Class | Namespace | Assembly |
|---|---|---|
| AddressFamily | System.Net.Sockets | System.dll |
| Cpu | Microsoft.SPOT.Hardware | Microsoft.SPOT.Hardware.dll |
| DateTime | System | mscorlib.dll |
| Debug | Microsoft.SPOT | Microsoft.SPOT.Native.dll |
| Dns | System.Net | System.dll |
| Encoding | System.Text | System.dll |
| HttpWebRequest | System.Net | System.Http.dll |
| HttpWebResponse | System.Net | System.Http.dll |
| InputPort | Microsoft.SPOT.Hardware | Microsoft.SPOT.Hardware.dll |
| IPAddress | System.Net | System.dll |
| IPEndPoint | System.Net | System.dll |
| IPHostEntry | System.Net | System.dll |
| OutputPort | Microsoft.SPOT.Hardware | Microsoft.SPOT.Hardware.dll |
| Port | Microsoft.SPOT.Hardware | Microsoft.SPOT.Hardware.dll |
| ProtocolType | System.Net.Sockets | System.dll |
| Socket | System.Net.Sockets | System.dll |
| SocketException | System.Net.Sockets | System.dll |
| SocketOptionLevel | System.Net.Sockets | System.dll |
| SocketOptionName | System.Net.Sockets | System.dll |
| SocketType | System.Net.Sockets | System.dll |
| Stream | System.IO | mscorlib.dll |
| Thread | System.Threading | mscorlib.dll |
| TimeSpan | System | mscorlib.dll |
| WebRequest | System.Net | System.Http.dll |

Secret Labs has created the following classes for their hardware, listed in Table B-2.

*Table B-2. Classes specific to the Netduino Plus*

| Class | Namespace | Assembly |
|---|---|---|
| AnalogInput | SecretLabs.NETMF. Hardware | SecretLabs.NETMF. Hardware.dll |
| Pins | SecretLabs.NETMF. Hardware.Netduino-Plus | SecretLabs.NETMF. Hardware.Netduino-Plus.dll |

Table B-3 lists the classes I created for this book.

*Table B-3. Classes specific to this book*

| Class | Namespace | Assembly |
|---|---|---|
| Buffer | Gsiot.Server | Gsiot.Server.dll |
| CSharpRepresentation | Gsiot.Server | Gsiot.Server.dll |
| DigitalActuator | Gsiot.Server | Gsiot.Server.dll |
| DigitalSensor | Gsiot.Server | Gsiot.Server.dll |
| HttpServer | Gsiot.Server | Gsiot.Server.dll |
| ManipulatedVariable | Gsiot.Server | Gsiot.Server.dll |
| MeasuredVariable | Gsiot.Server | Gsiot.Server.dll |
| PachubeClient | Gsiot.PachubeClient | Gsiot.PachubeClient.dll |
| RequestHandler Context | Gsiot.Server | Gsiot.Server.dll |

# C/Gsiot.Server Library

Here is a summary of the Gsiot.Server library interface. All items described below can be found in namespace Gsiot.Server, which is implemented in Gsiot.Server.dll.

## HTTP Server

### Class HttpServer

An instance of class HttpServer represents a web service that handles HTTP requests at a particular port, or uses a relay server to make the service accessible even without a public Internet address:

```
public class HttpServer
{
    public int Port { get; set; }
    public string RelayHost { get; set; }
    public string RelayDomain { get; set; }
    public string RelaySecretKey { get; set; }
    public RequestRouting RequestRouting { get; set; }

    public void Open();
    public void Run();
}
```

» int Port

Optional property that is set to 80 by default. If the server does not use a relay (see RelayDomain), this property indicates the port for which the server handles incoming HTTP requests.

155

» string RelayHost

Optional property, which is set to try.yaler.net by default. If the server uses a relay, this property indicates the address of the relay. If the server does not use a relay (see RelayDomain below), this property is ignored.

» string RelayDomain

Optional property, which determines whether a relay is used, and if one is used, what domain name is registered at the relay. By default, it is null, i.e., no relay is used.

» string RelaySecretKey

Mandatory property if a relay is used. The key is used for authenticating the device at the relay. The secret key is never sent over the network. If the server does not use a relay (see RelayDomain above), this property is ignored.

» RequestRouting RequestRouting

Mandatory property. At least one request routing element should be added to this property to support at least one request URI.

» void Open()

This method completes the initialization of the server. If a relay is used, it performs the first registration of the device at the relay. Before it is called, the server properties must have been set up. Normally, you don't need to call this method, since it is called by Run if necessary.

» void Run()

This method calls Open if it was not called already by the application, and then enters an endless loop where it repeatedly waits for incoming requests, accepts them, and performs the necessary processing for handling the request.

## Class RequestRouting

An instance of class `RequestRouting` is automatically created as a property when a new `HttpServer` object is created. Because it implements the `IEnumerable` interface and provides an `Add` method, it supports C# collection initializers. This means that instead of explicitly calling the `Add` method with the parameters `pattern` and `handler`, an initializer with `pattern` and `handler` as elements can be used (see Chapter 10):

```
public class RequestRouting : IEnumerable
{
    public IEnumerator GetEnumerator();
    public void Add(string pattern, RequestHandler handler);
}
```

» `void Add(string pattern, RequestHandler handler)`

This method adds a new request routing element to the collection, consisting of a request pattern and a request handler.

## Delegate RequestHandler

The delegate type `RequestHandler` determines the parameter (`context`) and result (`void`) that a method must have so that it can be added to a request routing collection:

```
public delegate void RequestHandler(RequestHandlerContext context);
```

## Class RequestHandlerContext

An instance of class `RequestHandlerContext` provides information about the received HTTP request to a request handler. The request handler uses it to set up the HTTP response to this request, and if necessary, to construct URIs to the same service:

```
public class RequestHandlerContext
{
    public RequestHandlerContext(string serviceRoot,
        string relayDomain);
    public bool ConnectionClose { get; set; }
```

```
    // request interface
    public string RequestMethod { get; }
    public string RequestUri { get; }
    public string RequestContentType { get; }
    public string RequestContent { get; }

    // server interface
    public string BuildRequestUri(string path);
    public string BuildAbsoluteRequestUri(string path);

    // response interface
    public int ResponseStatusCode { get; set; }
    public string ResponseContentType { get; set; }
    public string ResponseContent { get; set; }
    public void SetResponse(string content, string textType);
}
```

» RequestHandlerContext(string serviceRoot, string relayDomain)

The constructor of the class takes a parameter serviceRoot, which is the URI relative to which the request URIs are processed, e.g., http://192.168.5.100:8080. Parameter relayDomain indicates whether a relay is used; otherwise, it is null.

» bool ConnectionClose

Before a request handler is called, this property is set to true if (and only if) the received request contained a Connection: close header. If the request handler wants to indicate that it wants to close the connection, it can set the property to true, which will add the Connection: close header to its response.

» string RequestMethod

This property tells you which kind of request has been received (an HTTP method such as **GET** or **PUT**). You only need to check this property if you want to support several HTTP methods in the same request handler, i.e., request patterns with a * wildcard at the beginning.

» `string RequestUri`

This property contains the URI of the incoming request. You only need this property if you want to support several resources in the same request handler, i.e., request patterns with a * wildcard at the end.

» `string RequestContentType`

This property contains the content of the request's `Content-Length` header if one was present; otherwise, it is `null`.

» `string RequestContent`

This property contains the request message body converted into a string of text, assuming that the message body was encoded in UTF8. You only need this property for PUT and POST requests, since GET and DELETE have no message bodies.

» `string BuildRequestUri(string path)`

This method takes a path and constructs a relative URI out of it. If the request was relayed, this is taken into account. For example, `BuildRequestUri("hello.html")` may return */gsiot-FFMQ-TTD5/hello.* html if the request pattern was `"GET /hello*"`. You should use this method if your response contains relative hyperlinks to your server.

» `string BuildAbsoluteRequestUri(string path)`

This method takes a path and constructs an absolute URI out of it. If the request was relayed, this is taken into account. For example, `BuildAbsoluteRequestUri("hello.html")` may return http://try. yaler.net/*gsiot-FFMQ-TTD5*/hello.html if the request pattern was `"GET /hello*"`. You should use this method if your response contains absolute hyperlinks to your server.

» `int ResponseStatusCode`

This property can be set to indicate the status code of the response. The most important status codes for our purposes are:

```
200 (OK)
400 (Bad Request)
404 (Not Found)
405 (Method Not Allowed)
```

» `string ResponseContentType`

This property can be set to indicate the content type of the response. This so-called *MIME type* will become the value of the HTTP `Content-Type` header. The most important content types for our purposes are:

- `text/plain`

Used for a plain-text response such as a single numeric or text value.

- `text/csv`

Used to send a series of values.

- `text/html`

Used to send a response with formatted HTML.

» `string ResponseContent`

This property can be set with the content of the response message (message body). It will be encoded in UTF8.

» `void SetResponse(string content, string textType)`

This method takes a string and sets up the response message body accordingly. Parameter `textType` indicates the content type, e.g., `text/plain`, `text/html`, etc. This method sets the response status code to 200 (OK).

This method is provided for convenience so that status code, content, and content type need not be set separately.

# Resources

## Delegate GetHandler

The delegate type `GetHandler` determines the parameter (none) and the result (`object`) that a method must have so that it can be used for getting samples from a sensor:

```
public delegate object GetHandler();
```

## Delegate PutHandler

The delegate type **PutHandler** determines the parameter (**object**) and result (**void**) that a method must have so that it can be used for setting setpoints for an actuator:

```
public delegate void PutHandler(object o);
```

## Class MeasuredVariable

An instance of class **MeasuredVariable** represents a physical variable (temperature, door state, car speed, etc.) that can be measured by a sensor:

```
public class MeasuredVariable
{
    public GetHandler FromSensor { get; set; }
    public Serializer ToHttpResponse { get; set; }

    public void Open();
    public void HandleRequest(RequestHandlerContext context);
}
```

» GetHandler FromSensor

Mandatory property that must be set to a method that can be called for getting new samples.

» Serializer ToHttpResponse

Optional property that is set to **CSharpRepresentation.Serialize** by default. It converts a sample from an object to a string that can be sent as an HTTP message body.

» void Open()

This method completes the initialization of the measured variable. Normally, you don't need to call this method because **HandleRequest** calls it if necessary.

» void HandleRequest(RequestHandlerContext context)

When an HTTP request for a measured variable has been received, the server sets up the context object with the request information and then calls this handler. After the handler has completed, the server uses the response information in the context object to send its HTTP response message.

## Class ManipulatedVariable

An instance of class ManipulatedVariable represents a physical variable (temperature, door state, car speed, etc.) that can be manipulated by an actuator.

```
public class ManipulatedVariable
{
    public Deserializer FromHttpRequest { get; set; }
    public PutHandler ToActuator { get; set; }
    public Serializer ToHttpResponse { get; set; }

    public void Open();
    public void HandleRequest(RequestHandlerContext context);
}
```

» Deserializer FromHttpRequest

Mandatory property that converts a setpoint from a string that was received as an HTTP message body to an object.

» PutHandler ToActuator

Mandatory property that must be set to a method that can be called for setting new setpoints.

» Serializer ToHttpResponse

Optional property that is set to CSharpRepresentation.Serialize by default. It converts the most recent setpoint from an object to a string that can be sent as an HTTP message body.

**»** void Open()

This method completes the initialization of the manipulated variable. Normally, you don't need to call this method because HandleRequest calls it if necessary.

**»** void HandleRequest(RequestHandlerContext context)

When an HTTP request for a measured variable has been received, the server sets up the context object with the request information and then calls this handler. After the handler has completed, the server uses the response information in the context object to send its HTTP response message.

# Representations

## Delegate Serializer

The delegate type Serializer determines the parameters (context and content) and result (void) a method must have so that it can be used for converting a C# object (content) to the response message body in a context object (context):

```
public delegate void Serializer(RequestHandlerContext context,
    object content);
```

## Delegate Deserializer

The delegate type Deserializer determines the parameters (context and content) and result (bool) a method must have so that it can be used for converting a request message body in a context object (context) to a C# object (content). The Boolean result indicates whether the conversion was successful:

```
public delegate bool Deserializer(RequestHandlerContext context,
    out object content);
```

## Class CSharpRepresentation

An instance of class `CSharpRepresentation` provides support for converting any object to a string, and for converting strings containing Boolean or integer values to objects:

```
public static class CSharpRepresentation
{
    public static void Serialize(RequestHandlerContext context,
        object content)
    public static bool TryDeserializeBool(
        RequestHandlerContext context, out object content)
    public static bool TryDeserializeInt(RequestHandlerContext
        context,
        out object content)
}
```

» `static void Serialize(RequestHandlerContext context, object content)`

This method converts any C# object to an HTTP response message, basically by calling its **ToString** method. The special value `null` is converted to the string "null".

» `static bool TryDeserializeBool(RequestHandlerContext context, out object content)`

This method converts the strings **true** and **false** to C# objects. Other strings cannot be converted; in this case, the method returns **false** (**true** otherwise).

» `static bool TryDeserializeInt(RequestHandlerContext context, out object content)`

This method converts strings that contain integers to C# objects. Other strings cannot be converted; in this case, the method returns **false** (**true** otherwise).

# Drivers for Sensors and Actuators

## Class DigitalSensor

An instance of class `DigitalSensor` provides access to a pin that can be configured as a digital input:

```
public class DigitalSensor
{
    public Cpu.Pin InputPin { get; set; }

    public void Open();
    public object HandleGet();
}
```

» `Cpu.Pin InputPin`

Mandatory property that indicates which pin should be configured as a digital input.

» `void Open()`

Method that reserves the input pin, which must have been specified during initialization of the sensor object. It can be called explicitly, or automatically when `HandleGet` is executed for the first time.

» `object HandleGet()`

Method that returns the current state of the digital input pin as a Boolean object.

## Class DigitalActuator

An instance of class `DigitalActuator` provides access to a pin that can be configured as a digital output:

```
public class DigitalActuator
{
    public Cpu.Pin OutputPin { get; set; }
```

```
    public bool InitialState { get; set; }

    public void Open();
    public void HandlePut(object setpoint);
    public object HandleGet();
}
```

» `Cpu.Pin OutputPin`

Mandatory property that indicates which pin should be configured as a digital output.

» `void Open()`

Method that reserves the output pin, which must have been specified during initialization of the actuator object. It can be called explicitly, or automatically when `HandlePut` (or `HandleGet`) is executed for the first time.

» `void HandlePut(object setpoint)`

Method that sets the state of the digital output pin. It must be a Boolean object and cannot be `null`.

» `object HandleGet()`

Method that returns the setpoint that has been set by calling `HandlePut` most recently. It is a Boolean object or `null`.

## Class AnalogSensor

An instance of class `AnalogSensor` provides access to the current voltage value at a pin that can be configured with an analog-to-digital converter. By default, its `HandleGet` method returns the raw value, which is always between 0 and 1023 (10-bit resolution). If both `MinValue` and `MaxValue` are set up during initialization of the sensor object, a linearly scaled value between these two extremes is returned instead of the raw value: i.e., `MinValue` is returned for the raw value 0, `MaxValue` is returned for the raw value 1023, and values between `MinValue` and `MaxValue` are returned for raw values between 0 and 1023:

```
public class AnalogSensor
{
    public Cpu.Pin InputPin { get; set; }
    public double MinValue { get; set; }
    public double MaxValue { get; set; }

    public void Open();
    public object HandleGet();
}
```

» Cpu.Pin InputPin

Mandatory property that indicates which pin should be configured as an analog input.

» double MinValue

Optional property. If both MinValue and MaxValue are set up, this property determines the value returned by HandleGet when the analog sensor produces 0 as the value.

» double MaxValue

Optional property. If both MinValue and MaxValue are set up, this property determines the value returned by HandleGet when the analog sensor produces 1023 as the value.

» void Open()

Method that reserves the input pin, which must have been specified during initialization of the sensor object. It can be called explicitly, or automatically when HandleGet is executed for the first time.

» object HandleGet()

Method that returns the current state of the digital input pin as a double (64-bit floating point) object.

# Multithreading

## Buffer

An instance of class `Buffer` provides a threadsafe way of communication between actors (see Chapter 13). A buffer instance basically acts as a variable whose current value can be read and written:

```
public sealed class Buffer
{
    public void HandlePut(object o);
    public object HandleGet();
}
```

» `void HandlePut(object o)`

This method puts o into the buffer. The new value in the buffer replaces the old one. At most one value is buffered; there is no queuing of multiple values. The method performs the necessary locking to enable safe use of the buffer from multiple threads. Object o may be null.

» `void HandleGet()`

This method gets the current buffer state, *without* changing it. The method performs the necessary locking to enable safe use of the buffer from multiple threads. The result may be null.

# Index

## Symbols

@ (at sign), preceding verbatim strings, 118

{} (curly braces). *See* initializers; lambda expressions

=> (lambda operator), 91

% (modulo operator), 54

## A

absolute URI, 31

actors, with multithreading, 129–131, 136

actuators, 1

  drivers for, 165–167

  hardware for, 145–146

  server updating state of, 105–111, 118–119, 132–135

  writing to, 11–14

AddressFamily class, 153

AnalogInput class, 154

analog input ports, reading from, 22–26

AnalogSensor class, 100, 102, 166–167

API key, for Pachube

  obtaining, 38

  security of, 74

  using, 49, 51, 65

Arduino-compatible shields, 146

assemblies (.dll files). *See also* specific assemblies

  list of, 153

  .pe files translated from, 50

at sign (@), preceding verbatim strings, 118

## B

BlinkingLed program example, 11–14

boards, 146. *See also* Netduino Plus board

braces ({}). *See* initializers; lambda expressions

browser, as HTTP client, 30, 32, 35

Buffer class, 154, 168

buffer, for multithreading, 168

## C

cable modem, 44

cables

  Ethernet cable, ix, x

  micro USB cable, ix, x

casting, 55, 110

C# language

  delegates, 101–102

  initializers, 90–91

  lambda expressions, 91–93

  lock statement, 126–128

  methods, defining, 4

  modulo operator (%), 54

  test client in, 111–114

  type casts, 55, 110

  using directive, 13, 63

  while loop, 52

client. *See* HTTP client

code examples. *See* program examples

Concurrent Programming on Windows (Addison-Wesley), 136

Connect method, Socket class, 73, 82

contact information for this book, xi

ContentLength property, HttpWebRequest class, 65

ContentType property, HttpWebRequest class, 65

control applications, 35

Cpu class, 153

Cpu.Pin type, 14

Create method, WebRequest class, 64

porting to different hardware, 147–148
properties for deployment, 7
setting up environment for, 3–4
.NET Micro Framework. *See* NETMF
(.NET Micro Framework)
network address translation (NAT), 45
NMEA protocol, 145

# O

ONBOARD_LED constant, 13, 14
ONBOARD_SW1 constant, 14, 17
online resources. *See* websites
OutputPort class, 13, 146, 153
output ports, 13–14
Output window, 3, 8

# P

PachubeClient class, 154
Pachube service, 27, 37–41. *See
also* feeds
  account for, setting up, 38
  Internet address for, 45
  secure sharing keys in, 38
ParallelBlinker program example,
  132–135
parallel processing. *See* multithreading
path, in URI, 31
.pe files, 50
pins
  assignments for, 13–14
  changing assignments for a sensor, 138
Pins class, 154
Pins.GPIO_PIN_A0 to _A5 constants, 14
Pins.GPIO_PIN_D0 to _D13 constants, 14
Pins.ONBOARD_LED constant, 14
Pins.ONBOARD_SW1 constant, 14, 17
Port class, 153
port forwarding, 84, 95–96
ports, 94–96
  reserved, 94
  in URI, 31
POST requests, 31, 32
potentiometer, ix, 20, 21
  examples using, 20–26, 48–55,
    77–82, 99–103

reading from, 22–26
symbol for, in schematics, 23
as voltage divider, 25
Print method, Debug class, 5
process control, 98
processor boards, 146. *See also* Netduino
  Plus board
program examples
  BlinkingLed, 11–14
  EfficientPutRequest, 71–75
  HelloPachube, 48–55
  HelloPachubeSockets, 77–82
  HelloWeb, 85
  HelloWorld, 3, 4–5
  LedController, 105–111
  LightSwitch, 15–19
  ParallelBlinker, 132–135
  permission to use, xi
  ReceiveResponse, 75–76
  requirements for, ix–x
  SimpleGetRequest, 67–69
  SimplePutRequest, 61–63
  TestServer, 149–152
  VoltageMonitor, 97–104
  VoltageReader, 20–26
programs
  building as solutions in Visual Studio, 5
  creating as projects in Visual Studio,
    5–6
  deploying to device, 6–9
  embedded, v, viii
  erasing from Netduino Plus, 9
  running in debug mode, 8
projects. *See* programs
ProtocolType class, 153
public keyword, for methods, 4
pull-down resistors, 19
pull-up resistors, 18, 19
PutHandler delegate, 161
PUT requests, 32–33, 55–56, 61–67
  for manipulated variable resources,
    106–107
  resources changed by, 105, 118–120
  with efficient use of memory, 71–75,
    77–82

# X

# Y

# About the Author

Dr. Cuno Pfister studied computer science at the Swiss Federal Institute of Technology in Zürich (ETH Zürich). His PhD thesis supervisor was Prof. Niklaus Wirth, the designer of the Pascal, Modula-2, and Oberon programming languages. Dr. Pfister is the Managing Director of Oberon microsystems, Inc., which has worked on various projects related to the Internet of Things, from mobile solutions to a large hydropower-plant monitoring system with 10,000 sensors.

# Colophon

The cover, heading, and body font is BentonSans, and the code font is Bitstreams Vera Sans Mono.

# Buy this book and get access to the online edition for 45 days—for free!

**Getting Started with the Internet of Things**

By Cuno Pfister
May 2011, $24.99
ISBN 9781449393571

To try out Safari and the online edition of this book FREE for 45 days, go to **oreilly.com/go/safarienabled** and enter the coupon code TKMOZBI. To see the complete Safari Library, visit safari.oreilly.com.

## With Safari Books Online, you can:

### Access the contents of thousands of technology and business books

- Quickly search over 7000 books and certification guides
- Download whole books or chapters in PDF format, at no extra cost, to print or read on the go
- Copy and paste code
- Save up to 35% on O'Reilly print books
- **New!** Access mobile-friendly books directly from cell phones and mobile devices

### Stay up-to-date on emerging topics before the books are published

- Get on-demand access to evolving manuscripts.
- Interact directly with authors of upcoming books

### Explore thousands of hours of video on technology and design topics

- Learn from expert video tutorials
- Watch and replay recorded conference sessions

# O'REILLY®

Spreading the knowledge of innovators                    oreilly.com

CPSIA information can be obtained at www.ICGtesting.com
Printed in the USA
LVOW10s0037100115

422262LV00019B/762/P